HISTORY AND BIOGRAPHY IN
ANCIENT THOUGHT

LONDON STUDIES IN CLASSICAL PHILOLOGY

edited by

GIUSEPPE GIANGRANDE

Volume Twenty

HISTORY AND BIOGRAPHY IN ANCIENT THOUGHT

by

BRUNO GENTILI

and

GIOVANNI CERRI

J.C. GIEBEN, PUBLISHER

AMSTERDAM 1988

© by J.C. Gieben
ISBN 90 70265 49 4
Printed in The Netherlands

CONTENTS

Parce que l'histoire ne se fait qu'en se racontant, une critique de l'histoire ne peut être exercée qu'en racontant comment l'histoire, en se narrant, se produit.

J.P. Faye

PREFACE*

This book again tackles the problem of historiography and biography in the light of the various theories elaborated by the Greek thinkers on the structure of communication. This perspective also allows us to reexamine the earliest Roman historiography in its constant relationship with the historiographical doctrines of the Greek and with their narrative techniques. Such an angle has naturally led to an analysis of historical and biographical narrative viewed in relation to the readers or listeners for whom it was intended.

We are grateful to Prof. A. Momigliano[1] who read the previous edition of the first chapter of this volume and amply documented the practice of that public reading of historical works which is also abundantly attested by inscriptions of the Hellenistic-Roman period[2]. This practice explains still further the historiographical theories we have identified. They thus become even more intelligible since they were aimed not only at the reading public but also at the audience of these occasional recitals. We have never, of course, wished to deny that the principal means of diffusion to historical works in the ancient world, at least after the late fifth century B.C., was the book. Our purpose has been to throw light on the opposition between

*   With the exception of chapter I, which has been translated by David Murray, this book (*Storia e biografia nel pensiero antico*, Roma-Bari 1983) has been translated into English by Leonard Murray under the supervision of Proff. A. Hamilton, G.Giangrande and Daniele Guardamagna, to whom we would like to express our deepest thanks.

1) 'The Historians of the Classical World and their Audiences: Some Suggestions', *Ann. Scuola Norm. Sup. Pisa,* Class. Lett. Filos. Serie III 8, 1978, p.59 ff.

2) Cf. M.Guarducci, 'Poeti vaganti dell'età ellenistica', *Atti R. Accad. Lincei,* Cl. Sc. mor. st. fil. s.VI 2, 1927-1929, pp.629-665.

various historiographical tendencies which presupposed different narrative structures according to the various ways of conceiving and creating a relationship with the public, be it of readers or of listeners. The coexistence of the two types of communication is confirmed moreover by the continuous alternation in Polybius of the terms 'reader' and 'listener'.

A last preliminary clarification: the notion of orality which recurs in this book exclusively applies to the *orality of the communication* or the *aural dimension of reception*. To avoid possible misunderstanding we must emphasize that a correct usage of the term should be based on a rigorous distinction between three different forms of orality which may coexist simultaneously or which can exist on their own: 1) orality of composition (or extemporaneousness); 2) orality of communication; 3) orality of transmission assigned to memory[3]. In our analysis of ancient historiography only the second of these forms is considered.

3) Cf. R. Finnegan, *Oral Poetry,* Cambridge 1977, p.16 ff.

ABBREVIATIONS

Arrighetti 1977   G. Arrighetti, 'Fra erudizione e biografia', *Studi class. or.* 26, 1977, pp.13-67.

Bömer 1953   F. Bömer, 'Thematik und Krise der römischen Geschichtsschreibung im 2. Jahrhundert v. Chr.', *Historia* 2, 1953, pp.189-209.

Canfora 1971   L. Canfora, 'Il 'ciclo' storico', *Belfagor* 26, 1971, pp. 653-670

Cantarelli 1898   L. Cantarelli, 'Origine degli Annales Maximi', *Riv. filol. class.* 26, 1898, p.209-229.

De Sanctis 1953   G. De Sanctis, *Storia dei Romani* IV 2,1, Firenze 1953.

De Sanctis 1956   G. De Sanctis, *Storia dei Romani* I, Firenze 1956².

Dihle 1956   A. Dihle, *Studien zur griechischen Biographie, Abhandl. Akad. Göttingen* 3, 37, 1956.

Finley 1976   M.I. Finley, 'In Lieblicher Bläue', *Arion* n.s.3/1, 1976, pp.79-95.

F. Gr. Hist.   F. Jacoby, *Die Fragmente der griechischen Historiker,* Leiden 1954-1969.

Fraccaro 1957   P. Fraccaro, 'The History of Rome in the Regal Period', *Journ. Rom. Stud.* 47, 1957, pp. 59-65.

von Fritz 1956   K. von Fritz, 'Die Bedeutung des Aristoteles für die Geschichtsschreibung', in *Histoire et historiens dans l'antiquité, Entret. Hardt* IV, Vandoeuvres-Genève 1956, pp.83-145.

Gabba 1966   E. Gabba, 'Considerazioni sulla tradizione letteraria sulle origini della Repubblica', in

Gallo 1974 — *Les origines de la République romaine, Entret. Hardt* XIII, Vandoeuvres-Genève 1966, pp. 133-174.
I. Gallo, 'L'origine e lo sviluppo della biografia greca', *Quad. Urb.* 18, 1974, pp. 173-186.

Gelzer 1969 — M. Gelzer, in *Römische Geschichtsschreibung*, herausg. von V. Pöschl, Darmstadt 1969, pp. 77-120; 130-143; 144-153.

Gentili 1969 — B. Gentili, 'L'interpretazione dei lirici greci arcaici nella dimensione del nostro tempo. Sincronia e diacronia nello studio di una cultura orale', *Quad. Urb.* 8, 1969, pp.7-21.

Gentili 1972 — B. Gentili, 'Lirica greca arcaica e tardo arcaica', in *Introduzione allo studio della cultura classica* I, Milano 1972, pp.57-105.

Hanell 1956 — K. Hanell, 'Zur Problematik der älteren römischen Geschichtsschreibung', in *Histoire et historiens dans l'antiquité, Entret. Hardt* IV, Vandoeuvres-Genève 1956, pp. 149-170.

Havelock 1963 — E. A. Havelock, *Preface to Plato*, Oxford 1963.

Hölscher, 1973 — T. Hölscher, *Griechische Historienbilder des 5. und 4. Jahrhunderts v. Chr.*, Würzburg 1973.

La Penna 1967 — A. La Penna, 'Storiografia di senatori e storiografia di letterati', *Problemi* 2, 1967, pp.57-63; 3, 1967, pp.118-124; 4/5, 1967, pp. 187-195.

Latte 1956 — K. Latte, 'Die Anfänge der griechischen Geschichtsschreibung', in *Histoire et historiens dans l'antiquité, Entret. Hardt* IV, Vandoeuvres-Genève 1956, pp.1-37.

Leo 1901 — F. Leo, *Die griechisch-römische Biographie nach ihrer literarischen Form*, Leipzig 1901.

Leo 1913 — F. Leo, *Geschichte der römischen Literatur*

	I, Berlin 1913.
Levi 1963	M.A. Levi, 'La critica di Polibio a Timeo', in *Miscellanea di studi alessandrini in memoria di A. Rostagni,* Torino 1963, pp. 195-202.
Mazzarino 1966	S. Mazzarino, *Il pensiero storico classico* I-II, Bari 1966.
Misch 1950	G. Misch, *A History of Autobiography in Antiquity* I-II, London 1950 = *Geschichte der Autobiographie* I 1-2, Bern 1949[3].
Momigliano 1966	A. Momigliano, *Terzo contributo alla storia degli studi classici e del mondo antico* I, Roma 1966.
Momigliano 1974	A. Momigliano, *Lo sviluppo della biografia greca,* Torino 1974.
Musti 1970	D. Musti, 'Tendenze nella storiografia romana e greca su Roma arcaica. Studi su Livio e Dionigi d'Alicarnasso', *Quad. Urb.* 10, 1970.
Osley 1946	A.S. Osley, 'Greek Biography before Plutarch', *Greece a. Rome* 15, 1946, pp. 7-20.
Pareti 1952	L. Pareti, *Storia di Roma* I, Torino 1952.
Peruzzi 1970	E. Peruzzi, *Origini di Roma* I, Firenze 1970.
Peruzzi 1973	E. Peruzzi, *Origini di Roma* II, Bologna 1973.
Peter 1914	H. Peter, *Historicorum Romanorum reliquiae* I, Leipzig 1914[2].
Pfeiffer 1968	R. Pfeiffer, *History of Classical Scholarship,* Oxford 1968.
Strasburger 1968	H. Strasburger, *Die Wesensbestimmung der Geschichte durch die antike Geschichtsschreibung,* Wiesbaden 1968[2].
Till 1949/50	R. Till, 'Sempronius Asellio', *Würzburger Jahrb. f. Altertumswiss.* 4, 1949/50, pp. 330-334.
Walbank 1945	F.W. Walbank, 'Polybius, Philinus and the First Punic War', *Class. Quart.* 39, 1945,

pp.1-18.

Walbank 1957   F.W. Walbank, *A Historical Commentary on Polybius* I, Oxford 1957.

Walbank 1967   F.W. Walbank, *A Historical Commentary on Polybius* II, Oxford 1967.

CHAPTER I

THEORIES OF HISTORICAL NARRATIVE

It has been observed that the discovery of the historical dimension of man was, for the Greeks, a poetic one[1]: as early as the seventh century B.C. the elegiac poet Mimnermus of Colophon, narrating the colonization of his native town and the wars which followed it, interpreted the misadventures of the present as expiation of ancient guilt, according to a principle of divinely imposed causality which tended to re-establish order in human affairs[2]. More generally, a recurrent element in archaic Greek poetry was the recounting of remote history together with recent and even contemporary events (the colonization of cities, wars, civil and political strife) in which, at times, the poet himself had been protagonist with a strongly partisan spirit. This was a pragmatic poetry, directly involved in the real problems of its own society but, at the same time, seeking to indicate its political-historical antecedents by recalling the past[3]. The sense of difference and the awareness of continuity — the two basic components of historical thought — were in fact, as the poetry of Homer and Hesiod clearly shows, already an acquired element of archaic Greek culture in its bi-polar conception of the two great epochs of mankind — that of heroes or demi-gods and that of men[4] — a division according to which the

1. Cf. Mazzarino 1966, I p. 38 ff.
2. Fr. 3 Gent.-Pr.: cf. Mazzarino 1966, *loc. cit.*
3. For a fuller treatment see Gentili 1972, p. 57 ff. A survey of elements of historical narrative in archaic poetry has been attempted by F. Lasserre, 'L'historiographie grecque à l'époque archaïque', *Quad. d. storia* 4, 1976, p. 113 ff.
4. Hom. *Il.* 12,23; Hes. *Op.* 160; frr. 1; 204, 97 ff. Merk.-West. Cf. Latte 1956, p. 3 f.

heroic past, notwithstanding the uniqueness inherent in its character of factual reality, had to constitute the archetypical model for the present, almost in a perennial return to the mythical and exemplary age of the origins. This mental attitude, although recognizing the importance of chance and diversity in man's actions and thoughts[5], does not emphasize in a historical event what is linear, unrepeatable and specific, but transforms it into a mythological category, according to a conception which tends to be cyclic, and which represents the meanings and aims of human history by ways of a constant relation between present history and the mythical world of its origins[6]. It is such a polarization which, even in the plurality of directions and tendencies, was destined to mould Greek historical thought, and to reappear with new clarity and force in the Roman historians of the archaic age[7].

Within the area of this basic approach the two fundamental problems of all ancient history are to be found: first, the problem of the causal link between past and present, and therefore

5. One may think of the notion of 'chance' (*symphorḗ, týchē*), which recurs in the Greek historians and, for the idea of diversity, that is that "no day produces one event similar to another" or that the thoughts of men are always changing, see Herodt. 1, 32; Archil. frr. 131-132 West = 107-108 Tard.; Pind. *Nem.* 6,6, *Pyth.* 8, 95 ff. On the sense of *ephḗmeroi* ("beings who change opinion every day") in the last two citations, cf. H. Fränkel, *Wege und Formen frühgriech. Denkens,* München 1960[2], p. 23 ff.

6. It is not opportune to go back to the old argument about the conception of time in classical historiography. It is certain that excessively rigid schematizing led to the idea of a sharp contrast between the cyclic conception of time in Greek thought and the linear conception of the Judeo-Christian cultural tradition, which is not corroborated by the complexity of attitudes of ancient thought. In fact, with the idea of "Historical Return" one sometimes associates even ideas relative to the evolutionary process; and above all the concept of "Return" does not imply complete similarity between historical events, but rather exemplarity, in the sense of "Return" to a mythical model in individual or collective behaviour and attitude. For a balanced and exhaustive reexamination of the problem cf. Mazzarino 1966, II 2 p. 412 ff.

7. The idea of origin still lives, although within the limits of a different conception of history, no longer cyclic but horizontal, in medieval Christian historiography. In particular, as far as regards the chronicles of single cities, cf. A. Carile,'Le origini di Venezia nella tradizione storiografica', in G. Folena, *Storia della cultura veneta* I, Vicenza 1976, pp. 135-166.

the search for causes, both remote and recent[8]; secondly, the problem of truth or likelihood: that is, of critical investigation ascertaining the veracity of the information which the historian acquires from oral transmission or written documents.

But it is just in dealing with the problem of causes that the contrast between two marked tendencies in the Greek historians begins to take shape. The legend of the Trojan war can be used by Herodotus[9] as a point of reference in giving reasons for the great dispute between the Greeks and the Persians, according to the same kind of causal link already noted in Ionic elegy, which showed that violence suffered must necessarily find recompensation in an equal and opposite action. For Thucydides[10] however, the return to that distant, mythical past of the struggle between the Greeks and the Trojans offers only a term of comparison by which to measure the greatness of the political and military proportions of the Peloponnesian war which was fought in his own time between the Athenians and the Spartans. Although keeping to a structural scheme which embraces the mythical past and the actual present, Thucydides finds "the real, but unstated cause", which made the war inevitable, at the political level, in the growing dimensions of Athenian power which had awakened fear and apprehension in the Spartans[11].

The discussion of truth and likelihood or probability brings the historiographic problem into the realm of the art of rhetoric and particularly of forensic eloquence, in the sense that the

---

8. "Causes" in the most obvious sense, in the sphere of a deterministic conception to which certain subtle distinctions of contemporary historiography, which substitutes the idea of "cause" with that of "function", are foreign. In other words, more than the problem of "why", we today are inclined to pose that of "how" a given event is inserted in the international logic of the situation. For more details on the concept of historical causality today see E.H. Carr, *What is History?*, London 1961, c.IV. On the idea of function and purpose which, in all sectors of contemporary culture, is substituting that of causality, cf. V. Therrien, *La révolution de Gaston Bachelard en critique littéraire. Ses fondements, ses techniques, sa portée. Du nouvel esprit scientifique à un nouvel esprit littéraire,* Paris 1970, p. 123 f.

9. 1, 1-5.

10. 1, 9-11.

11. 1,23,6.

historian, like the orator, must reconstruct the unfolding of events on the basis of testimony and evidence, which confirm the credibility of the declared thesis.

We read in Thucydides[12]:

> But as to the facts of the occurrences of the war, I have thought it my duty to give them, not as ascertained from any chance informant nor as seemed to me probable, but only after investigating with the greatest possible accuracy each detail, in the case both of the events in which I myself participated and of those regarding which I got my information from others. And the endeavour to ascertain these facts was a laborious task, because those who were eye-witnesses of the several events did not give the same reports about the same things, but reports varying according to their championship of one side or the other, or according to their recollection. And it may well be that the absence of the fabulous from my narrative will seem less pleasing to the ear; but whoever shall wish to have a clear view both of the events which have happened and of those which will some day, in all human probability, happen again in the same or a similar way — for these to adjudge my history profitable will be enough for me. And, indeed, it has been composed, not as a prize-essay (*agónisma*) to be heard for the moment, but as a possession for all time. [Translated by C. Forster Smith].

This programmatic affirmation, which expounds the criteria of a rigorous search for truth (or likelihood, where the control of the truth is not possible) and which lays the basis of the historiographic direction which Polybius, in the second century B.C., was to term "apodeictic," already had its antecedents in the Ionic historiography of Hecataeus of Miletus (6th-5th centuries B.C.) who relied on history, that is on his own experience and personal examination, for narration of facts and the criticism of myths[13].

Herodotus too, in setting out the results of his research (*historíēs apódexis*) always distinguishes carefully between information obtained by direct observation (*ópsis*) and information which he has instead derived from the words of others

---

12. 1,22,2-4.
13. Cf. *F. Gr. Hist.* 1 F 1; see Latte 1956, p.5.

(*lógoi*)[4]. However, in the latter case, although, as he himself states[15], he feels the need to report what he has learned, he does not feel obliged to believe it[16].

In Herodotus the premises both of the criticism of tradition and the theory of causes begin to be sketched[17]. But in Thucydides these hints of doctrine become the object of rigid and systematic theorizing, which goes so far as absolutely to reject any element which cannot be critically controlled and to adopt the idea of usefulness as the final aim of historical narration. The mythical and imaginary components present in the stories of the poets and in the prose history of the logographers were thus rejected in the name of historical truth as mere instruments of psychological pressure intended to attract the hearer[18].

But we must ask what in Thucydides' situation motivated this radical break with the preceding Herodotean historiography. The traditional explanation presents the age of Thucydides as the twilight of a still "primitive" type of mentality, when rationality in human thinking begins to be prevalent: this level of analysis presents a naive antithesis between the mythic and the logical mentality, which it views as successive moments in the evolution of thought. Such naiveté today seems untenable in the light of modern ethnological and anthropological research[19]. The explanation, if any, is to be sought in the field of the technology of communication and information and in relation

14. 2,99.
15. 7,152.
16. On the problem of sight and hearing as sources of historical information, see especially G. Nenci, 'Il motivo dell'autopsia nella storiografia greca', *Studi classici e orientali* 3, 1953, p. 14 ff.; M. Laffranque, *Rev. philos.* 153, 1963, p. 75 ff.; 158, 1968, p. 263 ff. The question should be reexamined in connection with the evolution of the technology of communication from the oral and aural phase to that of the production and diffusion of books.
17. Herodotus distinguishes between *próphasis* (the declared motive, the pretext), *aitía* (the real motive) and *arché* (the occasion, initial moment of military or political event): cf. J.L. Myres, *Herodotus Father of History*, Oxford 1953, p. 56.
18. 1, 21, 1.
19. Cf. Gentili 1969, p. 20 f.; Gentili 1972, p. 62 ff.

to the passage, which was under way in Thucydides' time, from an oral culture to one of written communication[20]. The analytical and rational method which Thucydide demanded in historical writing was not, in fact, applicable either to traditional poetry or to the history of logographers, because an oral culture, due to its direct, immediate relations with a listening public, has mental attitudes and means of expression which differ from those of a culture of written communication. In a predominantly oral culture there is an art of writing which, in its psychological aspect, can be said to aim, by means of clear and concrete language and through paratactic, not hypotactic, structure, at preparing attitudes of thought which are immediately perceptible to the hearer and arrest his attention. This is the stylistic structure which one meets in the fragments of Hecataeus[21] and the *Histories* of Herodotus, which were, in fact, composed for public hearing[22].

Thucydides' argument with traditional historiography, whether in poetry or in prose, appears in very precise terms in the clearly expressed criticism (1,22) against the hedonistic aim of oral narration, designed to amuse the hearer rather than for a rigorous investigation of the truth, as in his own historiography. This point of view also defines the aims and means of communication of his work, which is not composed for the brief duration of a public declamation before a passing audience, but to constitute a permanent intellectual acquisition based on the written word and careful reading[23].

---

20. Cf. E.G. Turner, *Athenian Books in the Fifth and Fourth Centuries B.C.*, London 1952; Havelock 1963; Gentili 1969 and Gentili 1972; G. Cavallo, *Scriptorium* 26,1972, p. 71f.; *Libri, editori e pubblico nel mondo antico. Guida storica e critica* a cura di G. Cavallo, Roma-Bari 1977², p. XI ff.

21. Cf. Latte 1956, p. 5.

22. For a correct interpretation of the ancient evidence for the public readings held by Herodotus at Athens and Olympia, cf. Canfora 1971, p. 659 f.

23. This is the sense of "my history is a permanent possession (*ktêma es aei*), not a recital (*agônisma*) intended for the momentary listener". The word *ktêma* is not only and exclusively a metaphor, but preserves the normal meaning of "property" in a concrete sense which is referable to any object, the possession of which is lasting and inalienable. But if such is the value of *ktêma*, its direct

It is difficult to imagine a prose style more alien from the structural means and requirements of a public performance than that of Thucydides. Compact, compressed writing, tending to implicit rather than explicit thought, characterised by a tight, logical concatenation, it is a style which had difficulty in finding an audience disposed to follow the thread of the discourse with pleasure, requiring as it does by its very character an attentive reader alone with the text[24].

This critical attitude with respect to oral culture can be placed on the same level as Euripides' condemnation of all the poetry of the past[25] — "gastronomic" poetry, to use a metaphor of Bertolt Brecht's — in the sense that its principal aim was that of delighting, with the pleasure of song, the public of a banquet or a formal feast, rather than the more essential one of freeing man from sorrow[26]. Later Plato's objection to the poetry of the past, analogous to the Thucydidean criticism, placed the accent exactly on the absence of a rationalistic analysis of experience and of an appropriately dialectical development of thought[27].

contrast with *agṓnisma*, which is the performance presented with the aim of obtaining success before a public, induces one to think that the account here deals with the opposition between the transient *hic et nunc* of the performance and the lasting existence of the account consigned to the materiality of the written word, that is the book: cf.T.Kleberg, *Buchhandel und Verlagswesen in der Antike,* Darmstadt 1967, p.4 f. Certainly, Thucydides, as has been shown (Canfora 1971, p.657), foresaw (1,22,4) that his work would be read in public performances, according to the traditional practice; but the important fact is that he was not interested so much in the moment of the performance, as in the usefulness (*loc.cit.*) of his rational account to those who, in the future, would learn by reading it. The term *ktêma,* referring to the material property of the book, has a significant comparison in the use of the Latin *monumentum,* which could mean any monument in stone or bronze, but also a literary work in prose or verse, in the materiality of its written terms: cf. among the many examples Cato, fr. 83 Peter[2]; Cic. *De or.* 1,46,201; Hor.*Carm.* 3,30,1; Quint. 12,10,51.

24. Dion. Hal. *De comp. verb.* 22,II p. 108 Us.-Rad. explicitly affirms that Thucydidean prose does not respond to the requirements of a text intended for public recitation.

25. *Med.* 190 ff.

26. For more details cf. Gentili 1972, p. 63.

27. It has been the special merit of E.A.Havelock to have clarified in a definitive way that Plato's criticism of traditional poetry expresses the requirements of the new culture of written communication which was asserting

13

A different and opposite direction, which today we would call anthropological and ethnographic, has its antecedents in Herodotus and generally in the Ionic logographers. The assumption on which this historiography works is that the activity of the historian, like that of the dramatic poet, belongs to the sphere of mimesis, i.e. the faithful representation of human life. In the introduction to his *History,* Duris of Samos (3rd-2nd centuries B.C.)[28], arguing against his predecessors, Ephorus and Theopompus, pupils of Isocrates, because they had not known how to express the truth of the facts with sufficient efficacy, pointed out that this failure was due to their lack of interest in the mimetic aspect of narration and to the pleasure which it provoked in the public[29]. Ephorus and Theopompus, according to Duris, had pre-eminently turned their interest to the "written page" (*gráphein*), ignoring all those delightful elements which spring from a kind of mimetic narration which represents, through the influence of the words (*hēdonē̆ en tôi phrásai*), the

itself in the second half of the fifth century B.C. In this sense Euripides, Thucydides and Plato are the bearers of a single, identical cultural message. All three place at the centre of their polemical propositions the rigid contrast between the usefulness (*ōphélimon*) of a rational account, and the pleasure (*hēdoné, térpein*), inherent in the practice of the performance. Thus for the first time that antinomy between the useful and the delight, which was destined to remain one of the typical characteristics of European culture, was outlined (cf. Havelock 1963,157 f.)

28. *F. Gr. Hist.* 76 F 1.

29. The meaning of Duris' formulation is clarified by a passage of Diodorus (20,43,7), from which it is evident that: 1) the aim of "mimesis" is the representation of the "truth" of the facts and of the pathos inherent them; 2) a historical account without pathos, which is the very substance of the facts, is, to be sure, still an "imitation," but one which falls short of the "truth." On the undoubted dependence of this theoretical declaration on Duris, cf. Ed.Schwartz, *R.E.* s.v.'Diodoros', col.687; s.v.'Duris', col.1855. The argument of Diodorus (Duris) regards the concept of the inadequacy of historical narrative, in that different actions which happened simultaneously are presented in an "unnatural" time sequence and not in their simultaneousness: therefore, an account which does not represent the truth of the situation in an authentic way. For more details cf. Strasburger 1968, pp. 79 and 85. On Mrs. Lefkowitz's misunderstanding of the passage in Photius (*Bibl.* 176 p. 121a 41) which introduces the quotation of Duris' phrase, cf. B. Gentili-G. Cerri, *Quad. Urb.* n.s. 21 (50), 1985, p. 136.

14

truth of human life. In other words, they had not felt the need for such a written word which could arouse in the reader the same delight which the spoken word awoke in the listener.

The nodal point of Duris' argument with the two Isocratean historians is in the distinct contrast between the spoken word (*phrásai*) and the written word (*gráphein*). The meaning of Duris' categorical affirmation that Ephorus and Theopompus were concerned only with writing is clarified by Isocrates himself in a well-known passage of the *Panathenaic* where the diverse activities of speaking in public and writing are compared: if one requires particular gifts of a psychic and physical nature — courage, polemical vigour, range and strength of voice — for the other aptitude for philosophical reflection, which can find its adequate and elaborate expression only in the assiduous act of writing, is indispensable[30]. Naturally, Isocrates, lacking, as himself declares, the natural, physical and psychic requirements necessary for public speaking (but perhaps also due to a deep-seated vocation), was obliged to orientate his choice towards the activity of writing. But recalling the examples of Homer and the tragic poets[31], he recognised however the validity of the spoken word and its emotional and psychagogic effects: a validity which naturally is developed at the level of delight, not at that of usefulness. But he proposed usefulness as the aim of his writing, in the sense that he tried to form an ethical-political consciousness in the reader through a rational development of the argument and the resources of a sober, flowing eloquence. This gives us elaborate writing, contrary to all psychagogic effects, but perfectly aware of its efficacy, characterized by long, solemn, harmoniously constructed sentences. As prose it is elegant and artistic, but sometimes monotonous and dull, intended mainly to scan the logical articulation of the thought with its rhythm. In short, "graphic" not "agonistic" eloquence, as Aristotle was to say, contrasting in his rhetorical doctrine the structures and functions of oral narration and the quite dif-

30. *Panath.*10-11.
31. *Ad Nicocl.* 48-49.

15

ferent ones of written narration: not intended to express emotion, more "precise", more attentive in connecting thoughts and in formal elaboration, but less alive, too narrow and sluggish for the ear[32].

As we can see, Aristotle here is delineating a real doctrine of communication: it establishes the implicit, theoretical premise of the polemical attitude of Duris who, in fact, reproached Ephorus and Theopompus for having given to historical treatises the same bookish foundation which Isocrates' eloquence had shown[33].

Dionysius of Halicarnassus[34], in setting out the aspects and tendencies of Theopompus' historiography, offers precise elements of ascertainment, which confirm Duris' remarks on the bookish character of his work: the philosophical and moralizing arrangement of the narration, with frequent digressions on human virtues, long, accurate, solemn sentences, attentive to the correct balance of the images and to the rhythmic movements of the sentence, only occasionally pungent and biting, where the moralistic attitude of the writer came to censure human vices and passions.

Certainly, the psychological characterization of historical characters, the description of surroundings and customs and also every element which arouses wonder and amazement, represent an essential component of his work, which Dionysius

32. *Rhet.* 3, 1413 b ff.
33. In fact it is not possible to understand Duris' formulation, in all the implications which pertain to the foundation of the historical narrative and its formal aspects, if we leave aside the antithesis *phrásai-gráphein* and the exact meaning of *gráphein*, which raises the whole problem of communication technology and the terms in which it was explicitly described, as we have seen, by the culture of the fourth century B.C. This requirement, up to now, does not seem to have been noticed by the critics and, even when attention has been paid to the value of *gráphein*, as in the recent analysis, quite penetrating on other points, by Strasburger (1968, p.79 f.), the word has been interpreted in a more formal than substantial key, in the exterior sense of "style"; since *gráphein*, in the meaning elaborated by Isocrates and Aristotle, takes in not only the argument of rhetorical figures and tropes, but the very structures of thought, in relation to the exact requirements of written communication.
34. *Epist. ad Pomp.* 6, II p. 244 ff. Us.-Rad. = *F.Gr. Hist.* 115 T 20.

terms *polymorphía.* A *polymorphía,* the primary purpose of which was to be useful rather than to influence the reader psychologically, since the knowledge of the customs, both of the barbarians and of the Greeks, of the laws, of the constitutions, of the *biographies,* of the doings, of the objectives, of the chance vicissitudes of men, amplified and deepened the understanding of human nature and was therefore useful to the wide public of cultivated men, engaged in the various fields of intellectual activity, whether they were politicians, rhetoricians or philosophers.

This representational polymorphic aspect, as we have noted, also entails a type of mimetic narration, but not in the sense desired by Duris, a type of dramatic mimesis, capable of bringing the events narrated back to life, with all their emotional force, so as to transform the reader into spectator[35]. Thus the historian becomes, like the dramatic actor, the creator of a mimetic intermediary between historic reality and the public which experiences it, in a close rapport of sympathetic identification.

It is in this emotional and mimetic relation that historical *truth* appears[36], that truth which, according to Duris, the followers of Isocrates had not been able to reach, at least, we could say, had tried to unfold through an abstract, moral evaluation of people and events[37]. But, if the ethical truth of Theopompus had usefulness as its goal — the same educational usefulness which was the aim of the publicly orientated writing

35. B.L.Ullmann, 'History and Tragedy', *Trans.Am. Philol.Ass.* 73, 1942, p.25 ff., is right in recognising already in Theopompus a form of dramatization of history and, therefore, the introduction to a type of mimetic historiography, but he is wrong in thinking that Duris' orientation is the direct continuation of that of the Isocrateans Ephorus and Theopompus. Apart from some apparent convergences, which meet in their common ethnographical and biographical interests, the nodal point of the divergence is precisely in the different meaning and function which the idea of mimesis assumes in Duris' historiographic thought and practice. Cf. the remarks made by von Fritz 1956, p. 126 ff. on Ullmann's thesis.

36. Cf. n. 29.

37. Cf. Dion. Hal. *loc.cit.*

of Isocrates — Duris' mimetic truth performed the hedonistic function of arousing emotion in the reader and of pleasurably enthralling him in the narrative, a function which belonged to the spoken word. The notion of "pleasure" or "delight" (*hēdonē̃*) which words, joined with dance, gesture and song, can exercise on the listener, was one of the guiding ideas of all Greek poetry from Homer to the tragedians[38], and found its clearest and most explicit expression in the thought of Gorgias[39]:

I consider and define all poetry as speech in a metrical form. Into him who listens to it creeps a shiver of fear and compassion that induces tears and an intense desire which tends towards sorrow: before the happy and adverse fate of extraneous events and people, by the action of the words, the soul feels the emotions of others as its own ... The divine charm of the words awakens pleasure, banishes sorrow, identifying itself with the opinion of the soul, the power of enchantment betwitches, influences and transforms one with its magic[40].

38. The frequence of textual references does not permit an exhaustive documentation. It is sufficient to examine I. Latacz, *Zum Wortfeld "Freude" in der Sprache Homers*, Heidelberg 1966 and, more especially, Havelock 1963, p. 152 ff. and *passim*.

39. Fr. 82 B 11,9 f. D.-K. (II p. 290,20).

40. Regarding tragic "performance", Gorgias insists on the idea of the illusion exercised on the audience by poetry, presenting it as a mutual emotional rapport between the poet and the spectator: "he who deceives is *more just* than he who does not, and he who lets himself be deceived is *wiser* than he who does not" (fr.82 B 23 D.-K., II p.305,26). This interpretation was already suggested in the first edition of our book (1965) and also put forward by O. Taplin, *Greek Tragedy in Action*, Berkeley-Los Angeles 1978, p. 167 ff., who is one of the most sensitive scholars in dealing with problems of oral communication in tragedy. To understand the sense of this declaration, until now not completely understood, we must keep in mind that *díkē* and *díkaios* ("justice" and "just"), both at a cosmological level (cf. G.Vlastos, 'Equality and Justice in Early Greek Cosmologies', *Class. Philol.* 42. 1947, p. 168 ff; L.Sambursky, *The Physical World of the Greeks*, London 1956, p.8 ff.; J.-P.Vernant, 'Structure géométrique et notions politiques dans la cosmologie d'Anaximandre', *Eirene* 7, 1968, p.5 ff.) and at an amorous level (cf.B.Gentili, 'Il "letto insaziato" di Medea e il tema dell'*adikía* a livello amoroso nei lirici (Saffo, Teognide) e nella *Medea* di Euripide', *Studi classici e orientali* 21, 1972, p.500), imply the precise idea of equilibrium in the relationship of reciprocal actions amongst natural or human agents. The violation of this principle, in that it

But this relation of emotionalism, which established itself in the performance of a poetic text, would not be understandable without the idea of mimesis, which was at the base of Greek conception of poetic creation[41]: mimesis as bringing back to life through words, music, gesture and dancing, of a mythical or human action or a natural phenomenon. A mimetic process which transmits itself to the listener under the form of emotional participation.

But if pleasure becomes as one with emotionalism, which in its turn is related to mimesis, it follows that pleasure is one of the aspects or functions of mimesis itself. The relationship is clear from Aristotle's declaration on tragic poetry: "The (tragic) poet must procure, by means of mimesis, the pleasure which pity and fear arouse"[42].

It is clear then that "the pleasure inherent in utterance" (*hēdonè en tôi phrásai*) of which Duris speaks does not belong to the mere artifice of style which, on the contrary, characterizes the technique of composition directed only to the written word, but to the efficacy of the spoken word, in that it is the vehicle of expression for the mimetic message. In essence, Duris underlined the necessity for the written page to preserve the dramatic tension and concentration of the tragic performance — an undoubted transposition of tragic mimesis into the area of historical narrative. In this sense Duris is certainly travelling in the wake of Aristotle's *Poetics,* but with different theoretical connotations, in that he tends to identify the activities of the poet and historian in their means and aims which, on the con-

upsets a balance, is symbolized as an act of injustice (*adikía*), which necessarily brings a punishment intended to re-establish the norm of *díkē*. The "wisdom" of him who lets himself be deceived, that is, the public, spectators, is in his capacity to put himself on the same level as the poet and to take part emotionally in the situation proposed by the performance. The terms *sophía-sophós* still preserve in Gorgias the meaning of "ability", "capacity", "experience of an art", in this case the poetic art.

41. Cf. Havelock 1963, p. 20 ff.; B. Gentili, 'I frr. 39 e 40 di Alcmane e la poetica della mimesi nella cultura greca arcaica', in *Studi in onore di Vittorio De Falco*, Napoli 1971, p. 57 ff.

42. *Poet.* 1453 b; cf.also Plato *Resp.* 10,602c-608a.

trary, Aristotle[43] vigorously distinguishes, assigning to the first the task of narrating the "general" or what could happen according to likelihood and necessity, to the second the "particular" — what has really happened. But, once this identification of the two activities of poet and historian is declared, it is clear that the identification implicitly brings in its train a need that history too should have the category of the "general", which is, in fact, for Duris the mimetic *truth,* as a dramatic concentration of human passions[44].

In this antimony, between history as an account of the particular and history as individualisation of the general, are defined, in terms which today are still current, the duties of the historian as regards the facts, that is the problem of the particular and the general, of objectivity and subjectivity, which is as much to say the dialectical relation between facts and their interpretation.

This use of history, outside its complex, doctrinal relations with Aristotelism, had deep motivations in the cultural reality of the fourth-third centuries B.C. and precisely in the expressionistic tendencies of figurative art[45] and new forms of enter-

43. *Poet.* 1451 a-b
44. Von Fritz (1956, p.107 ff.) has the merit of having clarified in what sense the Aristotelean category of the general, inherent in tragic mimesis, operated on the thought of Duris, who was Theophrastus' pupil: in substance he has restricted Schwartz's thesis concerning Duris' dependence on Aristotle to clear and precise limits. The most debated problem (cf.e.g. F.Wehrli, 'Der erhabene und der schlichte Stil in der poetisch-rhetorischen Theorie der Antike', in *Phyllobolia für P.von der Mühll*, Basel 1946, p.9 ff., and 'Die Geschichtsschreibung im Lichte der antiken Theorie', in *Eumusia, Festgabe für E. Howald*, Zürich 1947, p.54 ff. = *Theorie und Humanitas, Gesamm.Schrift.z. antik.Gedankenwelt*, Zürich und München 1972, pp.97-120; 132-144), if the program of Duris reflects the thought of Aristotle or Isocrates, is in reality, as F.W.Walbank has rightly commented ('Tragic History. A Reconsideration', *Bull. Inst. Class. Stud. Univ. London* 2, 1955, p.4 ff.), a false problem, characterized by a non-critical schematism. As we have shown, the question is not posed in terms of the alternative, Aristotle or Isocrates, but in the more concrete terms of a problem with many complex cultural implications.
45. One thinks, for example, of the famous mosaic of Alexander which depicts a battle between Macedonians and Persians (probably the battle of Isso), found at Pompei in the House of the Faun, now in the National Museum

tainment, that is the new dithyramb and solo-singing. The expressionistic mimetism of the new poetry and music is clearly outlined, even in its technical aspects and causes, in the pseudo-Aristotelian *Problems*[46]; the introduction of solo-singing, without strophes, in contrast with the strophic structure of the chorus, and relying on the technical ability of a new professional actor, responded to the new need to express human passions in their authentic truth, no longer within the limits of that "conventional character" which had marked choral singing in fifth century theatre. With its tendency for psychological analysis of the characters and a type of ethnographic investigation, mimetic historiography found a suitable background in the political life of the Hellenistic courts of the Diadochi characterized by the determining influence of the personalities of the rulers and princes[47] and the view of the multiform world of the non-Greek populations of the Hellenized Orient.

But, in fact, in the contrasts of such a way of elaborating historical "truth", intended to represent human life dramatically in all its baffling complexity, resurface those very methodological instances of a rigorous, objective search for the facts and their causes which, as we have seen, had characterized Thucydides' historical thought. These are the terms of Polybius' (2nd century B.C.) bitter polemic against Phylarchus, a follower of Duris' historiographical idea, concerning his dramatic ac-

of Naples: a grandiose picture full of foreshortenings and efforts of colour, in which emerge, in a powerful dramatic concentration which does not neglect any detail of the scene, the psychological and emotive attitudes and reactions of the individual characters. Cf. A. Ippel, *Röm. Mitt.* 45, 1930,p. 80 ff.; G.E. Rizzo, *La pittura ellenistico-romana*, Milano 1929, tavv. 44-47; G. Lippold, 'Antike Gemäldekopien', *Abhandl. Bayer. Akad.* 33, 1951, tavv. 16,86; R. Bianchi Bandinelli, *Storicità dell'arte classica*, Bari 1973³, p. 323; *Il problema della pittura antica. Grecia classica ed età ellenistica e romana.* Lezioni del corso di archeologia raccolte da E. Faini, Firenze s.d., p. 100 ff.

46. 19, 15.

47. Cf. Latte 1956, p. 129 f. in his discussion of von Fritz's paper. To stress these cultural and political implications is not to underestimate the influence of Aristotelean theory on mimetic historiography (R. Syme on the observations of Latte 1956, p. 132). Obviously no doctrine simply exerts its influence without a cultural support which motivates its application and function.

count of the fall of Mantinea[48]:

In his eagerness to arouse the pity and attention of his readers (*sympatheîs poieîn*) (Phylarchus) treats us to a picture of clinging women with their hair dishevelled and their breasts bare, or again of crowds of both sexes together with their children and aged parents weeping and lamenting as they are led away to slavery. This sort of thing he keeps up through his history, always trying to bring horrors vividly before our eyes. Leaving aside the ignoble and womanish character of such a treatment of his subject, let us consider how far it is proper or serviceable to history. A historical author should not try to thrill his readers by such exaggerated pictures, nor should he, like a tragic poet, try to imagine the probable utterances of his characters or reckon up all the consequences probably incidental to the occurrences with which he deals, but simply record what really happened and what really was said, however commonplace. For the object of tragedy is not the same as that of history, but quite the opposite. The tragic poet should thrill and charm his audience for the moment by the verisimilitude of the words he puts into his characters' mouth, but it is the task of the historian to instruct and convince for all time serious students by the truth of the facts and the speeches he narrates, since in the once case it is the probable that takes precedence, even if it be untrue, the purpose being to create illusion in spectators, in the other it is the truth, the purpose being to confer on learners. Apart from this, Phylarchus simply narrates most of such catastrophes and does not .even suggest their causes or the nature of these causes, without which it is impossible in any case to feel either legitimate pity or proper anger. [Translated by W.R. Paton].

This page of Polybius forces itself on the attention not only for its polemical content but above all for the lucid synthesis in which he groups together all the theoretical aspects of the long debate on history as mimesis or as critical investigation, as art or as "science." The antimony between tragedy and history is to be seen in an elaborate system of semantics belonging to different means of communication and information, and thus to different thought structures and the different functions of the two types of narration. To the ideas (belonging to poetry in its oral contact with a listening public) of emotional participation

48. 2,56.

(*sympátheia*), illusion, likelihood, pleasure and momentariness, is opposed the truth, the usefulness and permanence of historical research which urges the intellectual diligence of the reader. It is a critical basis on which are united doctrinal motives already observed in Gorgias, Thucydides and in Aristotle and which confirms the sense of antithesis worked out by Duris between the spoken word (*phrásai*) and the written (*gráphein*)[49].

It is evident that Duris' and Phylarchus' historiography, as it aimed at a comprehensive representation of life in its multiple and varied characters, situations, etc., must necessarily have appeared to Polybius as lacking in that rigorous, unequivocal method which was the premise of his "pragmatic" and "apodeictic" history.

It is, therefore, a historiography "without method", this of Duris and Phylarchus, to which must undoubtedly be related the theory of Tauriscus[50], Crates' pupil, on the unsystematic character of the *historikón* or "historian" who deals with the *améthodos hýlē,* "a disordered matter", that is precisely a complex and multiform subject which is not susceptible to a controlled analysis by precise, methodical standards[51].

But it is just this absence of an unequivocal method, or at least of the method of Polybian historiography, together with the vitality of the existential content and the multiplicity of human interests which deprived this historiographical direction of reputation and reliability, so that it ended by being misunderstood even by the ancient critics[52], as a decadent tendency

49. The importance of Polybius' passage for the understanding of the *phrásai-gráphein* antithesis has not hitherto been adequately appreciated.

50. *Ap.* Sext.Emp.*Adv. math.* 1,252 f. = fr. 18 Mette, *Sphairopoiia,* München 1936.

51. In the passage, to which Sextus Empiricus refers, Tauriscus illustrates the three moments in which, in his opinion, the activity of literary critic is articulated: "logic", regarding the lexicon and grammatical tropes, "stylistics", on dialects and style, and finally *historikón*, on the contents of poetry and their mythological, historical, geographical implications — a subject for study, according to him, which cannot be reduced to a system, because, unlike language, it is not governed by methodical rules. It is the main merit of Mazzarino 1966, I p.484 ff. to have illustrated the implicit contrast between the Tauriscean conception of history and the apodeictic one theorized by Polybius.

towards romantic invention.

Plutarch's comment on the reliability of Duris' account of the return of Alcibiades to Athens is typical[53]:

Duris the Samian, who claims that he was descendant of Alcibiades, gives some additional details. He says that the oarsmen of Alcibiades rowed to the music of a flute blown by Chrysogonus the Pythian victor; that they kept time to a rhythmic call from the lips of Callippides, the tragic actor; that both these artists were arrayed in the long tunics, flowing robes and other adornment of their profession; and that the commander's ship put into harbours with a sail of purple hue, as though, after a drinking bout, he were off on a revel. But neither Theopompus, nor Ephorus, nor Xenophon mentions these things, nor is it likely that Alcibiades put on such airs for the Athenians, to whom he was returning after he suffered exile and many great adversities. Nay, he was in actual fear as he put into the harbour, and once in, he did not leave his trireme until, as he stood on deck, he caught sight of his cousin Euryptolemus on shore with many friends and kinsmen, and heard their cries of welcome. [Translated by Bernadette Perrin].

But whatever weight we may give to Plutarch's judgement, always so much against Duris' historiography[54], it is a fact that the representation of the scene, in all its theatrical solemnity and ostentation, is within the dimensions of the character, his ways and attitudes, as we can see from the biography of Plutarch himself[55].

In essence this mimetic historiography, in the importance which it gives to every aspect of human behaviour together with the individualization even of its irrational components, contain-

52. Cf. E. Schwartz, *R.E.* s.v. 'Duris', col. 1855 f.
53. *Alcib.* 32 = *F. Gr. Hist.* 76 F 70.
54. Cf. *Per.* 28 (= *F.Gr.Hist.* 76 F 67) where Duris' account of the taking of Samos by the Athenians is defined as false and tendentious.
55. Plutarch affirms, as we have seen, that the particulars reported by Duris are not reliable, also because they are not verified in Theopompus, Ephorus and Xenophon, the other historians who related the account of Alcibiades' return to Athens. In fact the argument is without value: precisely because Theopompus, Ephorus and Xenophon did not follow a mimetic type of historiography, they considered irrelevant certain particulars which had, on the contrary, great importance for Duris. Duris' account is confirmed by, amongst others, the fairly similar one of Athenaeus 12, 535 c-d.

24

ed in itself deep implicit needs which we today would call ethnological, psychological and sociological. It was an expressionistic historiography which, outside the methodological limits of a strictly political historiography, tended to represent directly the face of life. If its approach was alien to the aim of usefulness in a Thucydidean sense or the moralizing and philosophic usefulness of the Isocrateans, even it, however, followed a precise propaedeutic aim which is implicit, according to Aristotle, in the *tragic* representation of the passions.

But the contrast between the two types of historiography operated at the level more of programmatic intentions and expressions than of narrative procedure, if one considers the numerous indications of dramatic representations in those very historians, such as Thucydides and Polybius, who, from a theoretical point of view, rejected any concessions to a hedonistic and psychagogic use of history[56].

In the critical view which we have outlined here, we would like to emphasize the need for revaluation of this historiography, above all now that contemporary thought, even with the assistance of new methodology and techniques of investigation, has reopened the debate on what history is and on the task of the historian[57].

56. See Strasburger 1968, p. 80 ff. and recently J. Percival, 'Thucydides and the Uses of History', *Greece a. Rome* 18, 1971, p. 199 ff.

57. On the ever closer relationships which are being formed today between methods proper to historical investigation and those peculiar to relatively recent disciplines such as ethnology, sociology, psychology, etc., see Jacques Le Goff, 'Les mentalités: une histoire ambiguë', in *Faire de l'histoire* III, sous la direction de J. Le Goff et P. Nora, Paris 1974, pp. 76 - 94. For a theoretical discussion of the meaning and method of historiography, cf. also P. Veyne, *Comment on écrit l'histoire. Essai d'épistémologie*, Paris 1971. Veyne's theses, sometimes debatable and in some cases even paradoxical, are, nevertheless, stimulating and in a certain sense even provocative by the extent to which they challenge the conception of history as a science and the possibility of enucleating a real, precise historiographic method. Certainly, a very interesting position, but equally risky, at least in the terms in which it is defined by the author. When he declares that "ideas, theories and conceptions of history are unfailingly the dead part of a historical work" (p.144), he seems to want to relaunch, in essence, a certain model (which really is dead) of erudite and positivistic historiography.

Polybius' polemic did not exhaust itself in the contrast between his own method of historical investigation and mimetically orientated historiography: no less bitterly and more widely, with precise, critical interventions on method and contents, it attacked above all the Isocratean historiographic orientation, represented, as we have seen, by Ephorus and Theopompus. In the introduction to book IX of his *Histories,* Polybius, once again with severity and clarity, expounds the principles which distinguish his historiographical point of view from the predominant Isocratean one:

I am not unaware that my work, owing to the uniformity of its composition, has a certain severity, and will suit the taste and again the approval of only one class of reader. For nearly all other writers, or at least most of them, by dealing with every branch of history, attract many kinds of people to the perusal of their works. The genealogical side appeals to those who are fond of a story, and the account of colonies, the foundation of cities, and their ties of kindred, such as we find, for instance, in Ephorus, attracts the curious and lovers of recondite lore, while the student of politics is interested in the doings of nations, cities and monarchs. As I have confined my attention to these last matters and as my whole work treats of nothing else, it is, as I say, adapted to only one sort of reader, and its perusal will have no attraction for the large number. [Translated by W.R. Paton].

Thus, Polybius' history is essentially "pragmatic", limited, that is, by political events and excluding any discussion of an ethnographic or anthropological type which pertains to legendary traditions and to the founding of cities and colonies[58], those very events preferred above all by the Isocratean type of historian. It is an account which concentrates completely on the stating of contemporary facts and is thus always new and always different since it does not deal with the past, but with the present and, consequently, cannot draw on the statements of preceding historiographical models[59]. In defining the aim of his method of working, Polybius follows in the wake of Thucydides with a

58. Pol. 9,2.
59. *Ibid.*

rigid contrast between the usefulness (*ōphélimon*) of his own history and the pleasure (*térpsis*) which Isocratean historiography arouses in its readers.

But the terms of this polemic are specified with greater vividness and documentation in the very part of his work where he subjects to sharp criticism the work of his great predecessor, Timaeus of Tauromenium (4th-3rd centuries B.C.) who had related the adventures of the Greek West down to the beginning of the first Punic War: just where, in fact, Polybius' narrative began. The dominant themes of Timaeus' work, as can be deduced from the critical writings of Polybius himself, were the same as those which had characterized Isocratean historiography: colonies, foundings of cities, relationships, family histories, geographical digressions and the customs of different peoples[60]. That Timaeus' writings were characterized by Isocratean rules is explicitly stated by Dionysius of Halicarnassus[61] and indirectly confirmed by the judgment of Cicero on their "graphic" and not "agonistic" character[62], a point which is precisely verified in Duris' polemic against Ephorus and Theopompus whose interest was in *gráphein* rather than *phrásai*[63].

But other elements of structure and form also bring Timaeus back to the Isocratean way, through the frigidity of his writing, the prolixity of his account and that marked tendency towards philosophical reflection and sententious aphoristic language[64] which Polybius[65] bitterly censured, not so much for an aprioristic foreclosing as for a claimed superficiality or speculative incapacity on the part of Timaeus.

---

60. Pol. 12,26 d. On Timaeus, see Momigliano 1966, p. 23 ff. (with bibliography).

61. *De din.* 8 = *F.Gr. Hist.* 566 T 22

62. *De or.*2,14,58 = *F.Gr.Hist.* 566 T 20: *magnam eloquentiam ad scribendum attulit sed nullum usum forensem.*

63. Cf. pp. 15 and 105 sg.

64. Cic. *Brut.* 95,325 = *F.Gr. Hist.* 566 T 21; Dion. Hal. *loc.cit.*; Anon.*De Subl.* 4 = *F.Gr.Hist.* 566 T 23.

65. 12,25,6.

But, leaving aside every other aspect of Polybius' polemic on real or presumed historical and geographical errors[66], our aim is now to examine his basic objection to the bias inherent in the attitude of Timaeus' historical writings which mirrored the essentially propagandist aim of Isocratean publicity. This use of history tends to demonstrate a thesis and operates, therefore, like oratory, with the criterion of "probability" and not with the criterion of the truth, that is, that "truth" without which history, according to Polybius, becomes a vain and useless narrative[67].

In fact, Polybius, from his point of view, accuses Timaeus of falsifying historical truth not only due to the lack of direct knowledge of the places he deals with, the bookish attitude of his work, and because he has no real experience of any form of activity, public or private[68], but also and above all because he deliberately lies. Thus, with reference to Locri Epizephirii he observes, in the manipulation of the facts, that probability is a simple trick to disguise wilful lies[69]:

Timaeus frequently makes false statements. He appears to me not to be in general uninformed about such matters, but his judgment to be darkened by prejudice, and when he once sets himself to blame or praise anyone he forgets everything and departs widely from his duty as historian ... I am even ready to concede that Timaeus' account is more probable [than Aristotle's one]. But is this a reason why a historical writer whose statements seem lacking in probability must submit to listen to every term of contumely and almost to be put on trial for his life? Surely not. For those, as I said, who make false statements owing to error should meet with kind correction and forgiveness, but those who lie deliberately deserve an implacable accuser. [Translated by W.R. Paton].

But the discussion on truth and likelihood still merits some

---

66. 12,3 ff.
67. Pol. 1,14; cf.12,12. For a precise and lucid analysis of the Isocrateanism implicit in Timaeus' "tendentiousness", see Levi 1963, p. 195 ff.
68. Pol. 12,25d, e, g, h; 27;28.
69. 12,7.

comments. If Ephorus had denied that epideictic oratory required more attention, diligence and preparation than historical works[70], Timaeus, specifying the terms of this distinction, put the accent on the superiority of history with an analogical argument[71] which clearly presupposes the Platonic theory of two different levels of mimesis in the field of man's artisan and artistic activities: the artisan, in constructing any object, uses a direct imitation of the idea of the object itself; the artist, be he painter, sculptor or poet, in finding the contents of his artistic function, makes, in his turn, an imitation of an imitation, that is, he reproduces the object of an artisan which is itself the reproduction of an idea[72]. For Timaeus there is an identical relationship between historical and epideictic narrative, which he compares respectively to the real constructions and furnishings which are the work of the artisan, and to figurative constructions and furnishings in pictorial art. This is an argument conducted along the lines of the distinction between one mimesis as a perfect reproduction of reality and a second mimesis which, like *skiagraphía*[73] and scene-painting[74], creates a perspective illusion by deforming reality, in that distant objects are represented as being small and the nearer ones as large: an art, this, of illusion, that is to say, an art of deceptive likelihood.

The polemic attacks, which Plato makes against poetry, in the tenth book of the *Republic*[75], emerge with sufficient clarity from his own theory of poetry conceived, like figurative art, as mimesis. There are three arts which exist of each object: the one which uses it, the one which manufactures it, the one which imitates it[76]. Painting and poetry, the former directed to the sight, the latter to the hearing, are pre-eminently imitative arts. But imitative activity does not involve knowledge of the objects im-

70. *Ap.* Pol. 12,28,8-9 = *F.Gr.Hist.* 70 F 111.
71. *Ap.* Pol. 12,28a = *F.Gr.Hist.* 566 F 7.
72. Plat. *Resp.* 10,597 ff.; 602c; *Soph.* 233b ff.
73. Plat. *Resp.* 10,602d.
74. Tim. *loc.cit.* n. 71.
75. 595a-607a.
76. 601d.

itated: the painter, for example, does not know how to discern whether the object he is painting is well made or not, nor has any experience or correct opinion of it. Imitation is really only a pastime or a game since it is two degrees removed from nature and does not create true reality but only its appearance or likeness. In portraying an object, the painter accomplishes a second degree mimesis in as much as he reproduces an objective reality which, in its turn, is a reproduction of the idea of the object itself through the work of the craftsman. He works on the thread of the reproduction of reality and a second mimesis which creates the illusion of perspective by means of the deformation of reality; representing distant things smaller and closer things larger, or using tricks of colour to represent objects folded or erect, concave or convex (chiaroscuro painting, *skia-graphía*)[77]. It is therefore an art of deceptive probability intimately linked to that part of us which is contrary to reason and which has no aim be it healthy or true. By means of chromatic artifices it upsets the soul of the beholder.

The activity of the poet, the craftsman of images[78], is analogous[78]. His mimetic creation is also two degrees removed from reality. He does not understand what is, but what appears to be; he only creates appearances of actions, of virtues and of everything else. If he had a knowledge of reality he would create rather than imitate, he would prefer to be the object rather than the author of a eulogy.

Within the suggestive power of meter, rhythm and music, the poet exercises the same seduction on the hearers that the painter communicates through figures and colours, so great is the natural fascination which these expressive means transmit. Stripped of its ornaments and colours, poetry is nothing more than pure and simple words[79].

But what are the actions at which poetic mimesis is aimed? Those actions, compulsory or voluntary, as a result of which

77. 602d.
78. 599d.
79. 601b; cf. *Gorg.* 502 c.

30

men consider themselves happy or unhappy, become sad or joyous. For, like the painter, the poet is naturally inclined to imitate that part of us which is unreasonable (*alógiston*), senseless and base and which has nothing healthy or true about it. He imitates all the painful or pleasant appetites of the soul that accompany our every action and lend themselves to numerous different imitations, whereas it is not easy to imitate the wise, tranquil, uniform character, nor, if imitated, can it be easily understood by the heterogeneous audience at a feast or a theatre. It is, therefore, evident that the poet does not have a natural propension for the rational part of the soul and is not even inclined to satisfy it if he wishes to obtain the assent of the crowd.

That of the poet-imitator is consequently a harmful art because it insinuates in each of us "an evil constitution, satisfying the senseless part of the soul, that is incapable of discerning more from less and judges now great and then small the same things, creating fantasms, and is very distant from the true"[80]. An art of deception, it is only capable of arousing passions in the listener through the pleasure of song and gesture and of involving him emotionally in the mimetic sphere of the story. Welcoming the pleasing muse of poetry, the state will entrust its power to pleasure and pain instead of to law and reason[81]. The cletic hymn to the gods and the song of praise for the brave are the only poetic forms that the state will be able to acknowledge for they do not involve an imitation of reality and consequently do not damage the citizen[82].

But this scheme of arguments, according to Polybius, turns back against Timaeus, since faithful reproduction of reality could not consist, as he declared, in the onerous task of the collection and study of the sources necessary for his historical narration, but rather in direct acquaintance with the places and personal experience of the situations[83].

80. 605 d.
81. 607 a.
82. Cf. *Leg*. 7, 801c-802a.
83. 12,28a,6

In my opinion the difference between real buildings and scene-paintings or between history and declamatory speech-making is not so great as is, in the case of all works, the difference between an account founded on participation, active or passive, in the occurrences and one composed from report and the narratives of others. [Translated by W.R. Paton].

Exactly in Timaeus' bookish technique of constructing a historical argument Polybius recognizes a reason even for involuntary errors; and on the occasion when Timaeus approaches the truth it is always an artificial rather than real truth. He works like "those painters who reproduce straw models": their exterior design coincides with the real one, but is not capable of rendering the vitality and animation of living creatures[84].

On the contrary, a historiography which wishes to adhere doggedly to the truth of the events which it relates must, according to Polybius[85], respond to three fundamental methodological requirements: the careful study and critical analysis of the documents, a visit to the places in question (*autopsía*), a direct knowledge of the political problems. It is a "pragmatic" (*pragmatikḗ*) historiography in content, inasmuch as its subjects are the political, military and other events of recent and contemporary history, "apodeictic" (*apodeiktikḗ*) in its method, in that it proceeds according to the principles of "scientific" demonstration[86].

84. 12,25h.
85. 12,25e.
86. It is necessary here to specify that the current use of the term "pragmatic" in the criticism of ancient historical thought is often equivocal: an equivocation which comes from the incorrect opinion that *pragmatikós* and *pragmatikḗ historía* imply methodological types of connotation in the work of Polybius (M.Gelzer, *Festschrift C.Weickert,* Berlin 1955, p.87 ff. = *Kl.Schriften,* p.155 ff.; cf. recently K.-E.Petzold, *Studien zur Methode des Polybios u. zu ihrer historischen Auswertung,* München 1969,p. 3 ff.). In fact, a semantic analysis, which is obviously impossible here, confirms the interpretation proposed by Balsdon *(Class. Quart.* n.s.3, 1953, p.158 ff.), by Walbank (1957, pp.8 n.6; 42) and by Pédech (*La méthode historique de Polybe,* Paris 1964, p.21 ff.), according to which *pragmatikḗ historía* describes, in Polybius, the history of political and military facts, in contrast with that of genealogy, foundings of cities, colonization, etc.; that is, it regards only the

Two opposite uses of history which are both aimed at the preparation of a man of politics, but in different ways and at different levels: one, that of the Isocratean, proposing precise political and cultural objectives to be pursued; the other furnishing all the rigorously tested tools of political craft, of which the politician must be aware when making decisions, if he is to avoid falling into the errors committed in the past. The first is a partisan propagandistic historiography and in this sense it too is faithful to a reality[87], the second programmatically "impartial" and "objective", not politically involved, precisely because it is orientated towards the elaboration of a useful technique for politicians whatever their particular and incidental aims may be.

contents not the attitude of historical narrative. In this second sense Polybius uses the expression *apodeiktikè historía* about history which conforms to the rigid principles of a demonstrative method. For further details on historical method and polemics in Polybius, see D.Musti, 'Polibio negli studi dell'ultimo ventennio (1950-1970), in *Aufstieg und Niedergang der röm. Welt* I/2, (J. Vogt gewid.), Berlin-New York 1972, pp.1114-1181.

87. We are not, therefore, in agreement with certain tendencies in criticism, which reduce Timaeus' historiography and in general that of the Isocrateans to a simple historiography of erudite intellectuals, totally free from political intentions.

CHAPTER II

ASPECTS AND TRENDS IN ARCHAIC ROMAN HISTORIOGRAPHY

Historical writing, characterized by meticulous research on pre-sent and past episodes in Roman history, starts with the work of Fabius Pictor and Cincius Alimentus in the second half of the 3rd century B.C. during the years of the second Punic war. Until then the memory of the past had been entrusted to the archives of the magistrates, the priestly colleges, and the patrician families, and was little more than a chronicle of facts which occurred from year to year. In these circumstances, the annals written by the Pontifex Maximum assumed the status of official public records.

But the direct confrontation with Carthage and the Greeks in Sicily after the first Punic war created a new situation in which Rome, by now a great power in the western world, naturally felt the need to provide its own interpretation of its legendary origins and its history which had already been the object of historical research by the Greeks[1]. The scarcity of testimonials

1. We do not propose to tackle the complex and debated problem of the multiple variants of the legend of the origins of Rome in the Greek tradition and in modern historical criticism. Besides the somewhat questionable work of J. Perret, *Les origines de la légende troyenne de Rome (281-31)*, Paris 1942, cf. the most recent studies: F.Bömer, *Rom und Troia: Untersuchungen zur Frühgeschichte Roms,* Baden Baden 1951; E.J.Bickerman, 'Origines gentium', *Class.Philol.* 47, 1952, p.65 ff.; E.Manni, 'Sulle più antiche relazioni fra Roma e il mondo ellenistico', *Parola d.passato* 11, 1956, p.183 ff.; A.Alföldi, *Die troianischen Urahnen der Römer*, Basel 1957; C.J.Classen, 'Zur Herkunft der Sage von Romulus und Remus', *Historia* 12, 1963, p.447 ff.; Mazzarino 1966, I p.191 ff.; II/1 p.67 f.; Gabba 1966, p.133 ff.; H.Strasburger, *Zur Sage von der Gründung Roms,* Heidelberg 1968; J.Heurgon, *Rome et la Méditerranée occidentale jusqu'aux guerres puniques*, Paris 1969, p.223 ff.; K.Galinski,

and documentation does not of course permit us to measure the profundity of this research; there is no doubt however that, beginning with Theophrastus in the 4th century B.C.[2], interest in Rome induced Greek culture to acquire an ever more complete and precise knowledge of it, until, with Hieronymus of Cardia and still more with Timaeus, the Greeks recognized the decisive importance of the presence of Rome, which, after the victory over Pyrrhus, had become a leading force in Mediterranean politics[3].

The work of the first two Roman historians, Fabius Pictor and Cincius Alimentus, consciously placed itself in this tradition: their choice of Greek as the institutional language of historical writing, that is, a cultural language which guaranteed the accessibility of the work to the broader public of the Hellenized world,[4] was not fortuitous. This was a dialectical confrontation, in which Roman history undoubtedly adopted polemically independent views, but at the same time borrowed the institutional forms of historical narrative from Greek historiography. Moreover, a similar attitude in Hellenistic culture may be found in other non-Greek writers such as the Babylonian Berosus and the Egyptian Manetho (first half of the 3rd century B.C.) who wrote the history of their peoples in Greek, sometimes in open opposition to Greek historians[5].

Aeneas, Sicily and Rome, Princeton 1969; Musti 1970; Peruzzi 1970, p.26 ff.

2. See Pliny, *N.H.*3,57 = *F.Gr.Hist.*840 F 24a: *Theophrastus qui primus externorum aliqua de Romanis diligentius scripsit.*

3. Cf.Hanell 1956, p.150 and especially Momigliano 1966, p.44 ff., who attribute to Timaeus the merit of having first understood the new role of Rome in western history.

4. Cf. Cic.*Pro Arch.*23: *Graeca leguntur in omnibus fere gentibus, Latina suis finibus, exiguis sane, continentur.*

5. Manetho, for example, argues openly with Herodotus (*F.Gr.Hist.*609 F 13). For the parallel with Manetho and Berosus, cf. the acute observations of Momigliano 1966, p.61 and in *Histoire et historiens dans l'antiquité, Entret.Hardt* IV, Vandoeuvres-Genève 1956, p.172 f. Again, in the 1st cent.B.C. the Jewish historian Flavius Josephus declares (*Bell.Iud.* 1,1-3) that he is using Greek for the same purpose of making his own interpretation of the history of his people generally accessible, in contrast to those who had falsified the facts "either out of adulation of the Romans or out of hatred for the Jewish people".

It has been rightly noted[6] that, between the end of the 3rd and the beginning of the 2nd century B.C., Roman foreign policy had a concrete need to recall past events in propagandistic terms and above all to demonstrate to the Greek world the traditional good faith of the Romans in their relations with their allies as well as the purely defensive nature of the many wars they had fought. From a thorough analysis of the information we possess on the diplomatic activity undertaken in those decades it clearly emerges that one of the recurrent themes in the addresses of both Greek and Roman ambassadors was in fact the detailed discussion of the rights and wrongs of the policy of war or of alliance pursued by the Romans in a more or less recent past. When, for example, the propraetor M. Valerius Laevinus went to the Aetolians in 211 B.C. to persuade them to ally themselves with Rome, he felt the need to illustrate the juridical principles that had always regulated the relations between Rome and amicable national groups. To some of these the right of citizenship had been conceded, while others had preferred to maintain the status of allies (*socii*), so many and so great were the advantages connected with this qualification[7]. More than ten years later, at the outbreak of the second Macedonian war (199 B.C.), Macedonian and Roman ambassadors engaged before the Council of the Aetolian League in a proper rhetorical debate which was also historiographical. The Roman representative, L. Furius Purpurio, had to reply point by point to the accusation of the Macedonian orator who had conducted a close and impeccable analysis of the last half-century of history. His intention was to unmask the aggressive and imperialistic nature of Roman policy and to demonstrate how the Romans had always regarded the alliances and the defense of their allies as a mere pretext for military intervention in zones still outside their influence and thus as a means of subjecting them to their own dominion[8].

6. Gelzer 1969, p.79 ff.
7. Livy, 26,24,1-3
8. Livy, 31,29-31.

In this climate of distrust which threatened to spread over the whole Greek world and unite it against Rome while the latter was engaged first in the decisive struggle with Carthage, and later in a delicate policy of penetration toward the Eastern Mediterranean, it was natural that the Romans should feel the need for an organic reconstruction of their past history. This would permit them to present themselves to the other nations in a better light and to reply to the multiple and ever harsher accusations of which they were the object. Such diplomatic and propagandistic function of historiographical works also explains the use of Greek by the Roman historians at the time when Naevius and Ennius were celebrating the history of Rome in Latin verse, obviously addressing a very different public, the community of their fellow citizens.

Indeed, the history of the first Punic war was written in Greek by Philinus of Acragas who, according to the testimony of Polybius[9], presented the facts from a point of view completely opposed to that of Fabius and openly defended the Carthaginian policy:

An equally powerful motive with me for paying particular attention to this war is that, to my mind, the truth has not been adequately stated by those historians who are reputed to be the best authorities on it, Philinus and Fabius. I do not indeed accuse them of intentional falsehood, in view of their character and principles, but they seem to me to have been much in the case of lovers; for owing to his convictions and constant partiality Philinus will have it that the Carthaginians in every case acted wisely, well, and bravely, and the Romans otherwise, whilst Fabius takes the precisely opposite view. [Translated by W.R.Paton].

Elsewhere Polybius[10], dealing with the causes of the second Punic war, shows up Fabius' aptitude still more clearly:

Fabius, the Roman annalist, says that besides the outrage on the Saguntines, a cause of the war was Hasdrubal's ambition and love of

9. 1,14,1-3 = Fab.Pict.fr.21 Peter² = *F.Gr.Hist.*809 T 6a.
10. 3,8,1-7 = Fab.Pict.fr.25 Peter² = *F.Gr.Hist.* 809 F 21.

power. He tells us how, having acquired a great dominion in Spain, he arrived in Africa and attempted to abolish the constitution of Carthage and change the form of government to monarchy. The leading statesmen, however, got wind of his project and united to oppose him, upon which Hasdrubal, suspicious of their intentions, left Africa and in future governed Iberia as he chose, without paying any attention to the Carthaginian Senate. Hannibal from boyhood had shared and admired Hasdrubal's principles; and on succeeding to the governor-generalship of Iberia, he had employed the same method as Hasdrubal. Consequently, he now began this war against Rome on his own initiative and defiance of Carthaginian opinion, not a single one of the notables in Carthage approving his conduct towards Saguntum. [Translated by W.R.Paton].

In open polemic with Fabius, Polybius denies that the cause of the second Punic war should be attributed to the initiative of Hasdrubal and the conduct of Hannibal: it should, rather, be considered as a complex convergence of various factors, among which the policy pursued by Hamilcar Barca, starting from the years of the war in Sicily, was decisive. If first Hasdrubal and then Hannibal had really acted in complete disagreement with the entire Carthaginian senate, we would be unable to understand why this latter body did not comply with the Romans' request, and surrender Hannibal, who was responsible for the acts of injustice committed[11].

Even without going any more deeply into the argument, it is evident that Fabius' simplification in his analysis should not be attributed to insufficient knowledge of the political facts, but to an evaluation of the events demonstrating beyond a shadow of doubt the injustice and the abuse of power perpetrated by Hannibal and the legitimacy of the ultimatum issued by the Romans. The bias given by Fabius to his argument effectively reflects that partiality towards the Roman point of view which Polybius had attributed to him when he placed him on a par with Philinus, a supporter of the Carthaginian cause. The charge of insuffi-

11. 3,8,8-11. On Polybius' quarrel with Fabius, about the cause of the second Punic War, and on the philo-Roman implication of Fabius' thesis, cf. the lucid and balanced analysis of D.Musti, 'Polibio e la storiografia romana arcaica', in *Polybe, Entret.Hardt* XX, Vandoeuvres-Genève 1974, p.120 f.

cient understanding of the historical facts formulated by Polybius with regard to Fabius should be considered in the general light of the controversy pursued by Polybius with his predecessors who had committed the error of not adhering to the methodological principles of his "apodeictic" historiography.

Even if he does not explicitly affirm it, Polybius' argument thus reveals a substantially propagandistic attitude in Fabius' narrative, an attitude that some scholars[12] have wrongly denied without providing arguments which invalidate the testimony of the Greek historian.

In fact, when we tackle the problem of archaic Roman historiography in the perspective of its institutional genesis and its methodological implications, we experience an unsettling disorientation with regard to the heterogeneity of modern criticism: that close-knit web of hypotheses and interpretations, in most cases undermined by a fundamental misunderstanding of what, already in Greek culture, were the real terms of a theoretical debate on the use of history.

For example, the search for "causes" in the Fabius fragment has led some modern scholars into error, inducing them to see in him a historian of a "pragmatic" or, rather, "apodeictic" tendency[13], a harbinger, in the field of Roman historiography, of the method that was later to be theorized by Polybius[14]. In Fabius we undoubtedly sense the desire to identify the genesis of

12. Bömer 1953, p.202; D.Timpe, 'Fabius Pictor und die Anfänge der römischen Historiographie', in *Aufstieg und Niedergang der röm.Welt* I/2, (J.Vogt gewid.), Berlin-New York 1972, p.931.

13. For the meaning of the terms 'pragmatic' and 'apodeictic', cf. Chapter I, n.86.

14. The two essays of Gelzer (1969, pp.77-129; 130-153), which had the merit of making a clear distinction between the earliest Roman historical writing in Greek and the pontifical annals, take for granted some theoretical propositions which, far from being acceptable, are actually misleading to the extent that they start with the presupposition that historiography different from the pontifical annals must necessarily be 'pragmatic' and that a propagandistic historiography would be *simply* a 'pragmatic' historiography. Gelzer makes no attempt to define the notion of 'pragmatic' historiography, a notion which always remains extremely vague in his work.

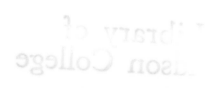

the facts by returning to the political motives of their protagonists. But in this case the quest for cause has a propagandistic function and is not inspired by the principles of the
apodeictic method. In other words, when Fabius Pictor was
speaking of the expansionist policy recommended by Hasdrubal
and Hannibal in opposition to the senatorial oligarchy he was
also seeking to show that the Romans had been forced to take
up arms to defend themselves from a war of aggression,
favoured by the Barca dynasty with precise objectives of personal power, but disapproved of by the more responsible classes
of the Carthaginian people. The search for "causes" was not an
exclusive result of Polybius' "apodeictic" method.

Fabius' deliberately argumentative message achieves a clear
and decisive increase in quality with respect to the tradition of
the pontifical annals. To understand this is not enough to identify the political reasons for a historiography different from a
pure and simple annalistic record, but we must also tackle the
problem of this new form of historical writing on an institutional level. The literary annals must be judged according to the
criterion of readability, unlike the pontifical annals which,
because they were chronicles, intended for the archives, were
not concerned with their relationship with proper reading public
(see Appendix I).

Some modern critics[15] have wanted to deny a discontinuity
between the tradition of the pontifical annals and the historiography of Fabius Pictor, Cincius Alimentus, and the others who
followed in their footsteps, initially using Greek and, later, with
Cato inaugurating Latin historical writing. Of course the lack of
any proper fragments of the original pontifical chronicle makes
it more difficult to reach any rigorously demonstrable or
definite solutions. However, while the testimony of Cicero, Servius and Cato[16] suggests a type of extremely concise report,
more like a list of brief propositions than an articulated and

15. Bömer 1953, p.202.
16. Cf. Appendix I.

organic narrative, a likely hypothesis[17] is that we can see a reflection of the narrative mode of the *commentarii pontificum* in some passages of the works of Livy, especially in linking passages in which the author limits himself to a succinct listing of the facts which he believes to be less relevant from the historical point of view.

This hiatus between the tradition of the pontifical annals and the historiography of the third and second century B.C. poses precise problems of a historical-cultural order, the solution of which is suggested by Leo[18]: "The style (in the pontifical chronicle) was undoubtedly brief and concise; there is no question of the diffuse and thorough narrative, which was only to arise under the influence of the Greek technique".

But we have seen how impossible it is to speak of a single univocal Greek historiographic technique and how several tendencies and methodologies coexisted which were not only distinct but controversially opposed to each other.

The problem of the earliest Roman historiography thus becomes identified with the need to determine which of the tendencies of Greek historiography had a preponderant influence on Fabius Pictor, Cincius Alimentus and the Roman historians of the second century B.C., before the teaching of Polybius made its innovating influence felt.

The Greek historian who first treated Roman history in more than a marginal way, and made it the principal subject of the narrative, was Timaeus of Tauromenium[19]. Significantly enough Polybius considered Timaeus his own immediate predecessor as historian of the Roman people: he refused to recount the facts already related by him and began in the year in which his work came to an end (264 B.C.). If Timaeus was the first to understand the part that Rome was setting out to perform in the political arena of the West, he presumably exercised

17. Peter 1914, p.XXV ff.
18. 1913, p.44.
19. The way in which Gellius,11,1,1 = *F.Gr.Hist.*566 T 9e, cites his work is relevant: *Timaeus in historiis quas oratione Graeca de rebus populi Romani composuit.*

42

a decisive influence on those first Roman writers who wrote the history of their people in Timaeus' own language. His was also a decisive contribution in that he offered the model of a historiographic structure different to the pontifical chronicle. We thus arrive at the hypothesis of a substantially "Isocratean" character of archaic Roman historiography, if Timaeus can really be placed in that same historiographic school which embraces the work of Ephorus and Theopompus[20]: a hypothesis which will naturally have to be confirmed by an analysis of the fragments, but which meanwhile tallies perfectly with the propagandistic tendency[21] of Fabius' narrative and with what has already been said about his search for causes in his pages on the second Punic war.

No one has emphasized with sufficient clarity that the identification of the reasons for historic events was also considered a characteristic of the historiography of the "Isocratean" school by ancient critics. The ultimate purpose of the etiological analysis, as in Fabius' passage on Hasdrubal and Hannibal, was the moral denunciation of a crime for which the protagonist of a political act is responsible. Dionysius of Halicarnassus[22] writes about the Isocratean Theopompus:

> The most characteristic element of his history, which is not developed with equal care and efficacy in any of the other historians, either past or present ... is the aptitude, while treating various political facts, not only to see and to say what is evident to everyone, but also to seek the hidden motives (*aitíai*) of the actions and of the man who accomplished them and the passions that agitate the mind, which are not easy to discern in the majority of men.

From Polybius' remarks on Fabius Pictor it clearly emerges that the causes of the war were attributed by the Roman

---

20. On the 'Isocratean' character of the narrative technique of Timaeus' work cf. p.27 ff.

21. On the propagandistic aim peculiar to Isocratean historiography and, in particular, on the tendentiousness of Timaeus, cf. the analysis of Levi 1963, p.195 ff.

22. *Epist.ad Pomp.* 6,7 (II p.246,6 Us.-Rad.).

historian to those very "passions that were agitating the mind" of Hasdrubal, to his arrogance (πλεονεξία), and to his boundless ambition for power (φιλαρχία) which Hannibal had profoundly admired and assimilated from his adolescence onwards. This analysis of the causes placed its stress more on the subjective and emotional components than on the objective reasons of a strictly political order with which Polybius was mainly concerned.

But if, from a narrative point of view, this early Roman historiography reflected the modes and the attitudes of Hellenistic historiography, the influence of the traditional chronicle material (besides the decisive contribution of the Greek historians who had concerned themselves with Rome) must not be underestimated. Moreover, though differing greatly from the bare listing of facts peculiar to the *Annales Pontificum,* the new historiography retained the annalistic form of the year by year report[23] and, like rhetoric, remained a literary phenomenon of the governing class which thus found an instrument suitable for asserting "its interpretation of history and political reality"[24] and for emphasizing the ethnographic aspects and religious values which it considered proper to Roman tradition.

Another feature that links Roman historical writing with its Greek model is that its object was essentially the origins of Rome and contemporary history. This relates historical writing to the epic of Naevius[25] and Ennius[26], as has often been pointed out. The events between the remotest origins and contemporary history received slight emphasis and were not developed proportionately to the rest of the work. The resulting polarization of

23. J.Vogt, *Gnomon* 12, 1936, pp.513-527 = *Römische Geschichtsschreibung,* herausg. von V. Pöschl, Darmstadt 1969, p.199, rightly observes, as against Gelzer, that the annalistic ordering of the material does not in itself exclude a historical narrative more complex and reasoned than that of the pontifical chronicle.

24. La Penna 1967, p.57.

25. See finally L.Ferrero, *Rerum scriptor. Saggi sulla storiografia romana,* Trieste, Università degli Studi, 1962, p.17.

26. Peter 1914, p.LXXIV n.2; Gabba 1966, p.133 ff.

historical interest[27] had already been noted by Dionysius of Halicarnassus[28] when he accused Fabius Pictor and Cincius Alimentus of only narrating "succinctly" the events following the foundation of the city. Nor did Cato's technique differ, for Roman history of the 5th and 4th centuries B.C. was given little to no space in the seven books of the *Origines*. The origins of Rome, the period of the monarchy, the origins of the Italic cities and contemporary history from the Punic war onwards were the almost exclusive subject of his narrative.

This historiographic scheme was variously justified either by the political vocation of the Roman historians, who were politicians and protagonists of the history they were writing[29] rather than writers, or by the hypothesis of an insufficient documentation for the intermediate period between the origins and contemporary history[30].

A different approach[31], but which only takes the cultural significance of the phenomenon into partial consideration, consists of comparing the practice of the Latin historians with that of some Greek historians and particularly of the atthidographers like Philochorus, the author of a history of Attica (*Atthís*).

27. Cf.Gabba 1966, p.135 ff.
28. 1,6. The same expression (κεφαλαιωδῶς) is used by Dionysius (*Opusc.*I, p.340,2 Us.-Rad.) with reference to the brief account that Thucydides gives of the *pentekontaetía*, that is, of the 50 years of Athenian history which elapsed between the Persian war and the Peloponnesian war; cf. Gelzer 1969, p.146.
29. La Penna 1967, p.58 ff.
30. Cf.Gabba 1966, pp.138 f.; 164 ff., who explains the lack of documentation on the first republican age up until the Samnite wars by the dependence of the Latin historians on Greek sources. According to Gabba, the main objective of Greek historical writing about Rome, which develops above all from the 4th cent.B.C. when Rome began to assume an unquestionable political importance, was to insert Rome 'into the framework of Greek history': for this reason it was almost exclusively concerned with the origins and the regal period at the expense of the 5th century and the first half of the 4th century. For the hypothesis of the lack of documentation, see also D.Timpe, in *Aufstieg und Niedergang der röm.Welt* cit. p.949.
31. Peter 1914, p.LXXIV; Walbank 1945, p.17 ff.; M.Barchiesi, *Nevio epico*, Padova 1962, p.202 n.1051a; Hanell 1956, p.165.

45

In reality this polarization reflects, as we have seen[32], a mental scheme that permeates all Greek historical thought: a conception that establishes a direct and immediate relationship between the world of the origins and the present through the paradigmatic value of myth. The mythical personage becomes a model of ethical and civic behaviour who, even in a social structure different from the Greek one, functions as a constant reference to the integrity of behaviour, frugality and simplicity proper to primeval times. Typical is the manner in which Piso Frugi evokes the human and behavioural aspects in the private, everyday life of Romulus. Gellius writes[33]:

Lucius Piso Frugi has shown an elegant simplicity of diction and thought in the first book of his *Annals,* when writing of the life and habits of King Romulus. His words are as follows: "They say also of Romulus, that being invited to dinner, he drank but little there, giving the reason that he had business for the following day. They answer: 'If all men were like you, Romulus, wine would be cheaper'. 'Nay, dear', answered Romulus, 'if each man drank as much as he wished; for I drank as much as I wished' ''. [Translated by J.C. Rolfe].

The first king becomes a symbol of that parsimony and integrity on which the political rise of Rome is said to have been founded. This model life was deliberately contrasted with the new customs which had been introduced into Roman society after the direct contact with the Greek East, but which continued to be regarded as a cause of inevitable moral and civic decadence. In the work of Piso Frugi, no less than in that of Cato, we find a denunciation of the laxity of customs, of the spreading of luxury, immodesty and lasciviousness of the young[34]. The paradigmatic relationship between the mythical

32. See p.7 f.
33. 11,14 = fr.8 Peter[2].
34. Frr.34; 38 and 40 Peter[2]. In fr.34 an explicit reference is made to luxurious furnishings imported from Asia in 187 B.C. by Gnaeus Manlius Vulso, on the occasion of his triumph. Livy too (39,6,7) places the beginning of the decadence of ancient morality in 187 B.C. A very precise allusion to this cultural panorama within which the new customs imported from Greece were

past and the present thus becomes coloured by a sense of mistrust of the present, through a direct awareness of a progressive and irreversible moral crisis. It then becomes the basis of a pessimistic conception of history due to remain one of the fundamental motifs of Roman culture[35]. This historiographical pessimism does not, however, exclude a faith in the destiny of Rome already present in the historical epic of Naevius[36] and in Fabius Pictor, judging at least from the meaning he attributed in his work to the very name of *Capitolium*[37]. It is an eschatological conception of history which does not clash with the genetic legend, but rather confers a value on it and sees in the act of foundation the beneficial roots of future events that will mark the progressive fulfilment of Rome's providential rôle[38].

From the outset, therefore, Roman historiography is characterized by a moralistic attitude, reflecting on the ethos of peoples and individuals, an attitude which brings us back to the "Isocratean" school of historiography. Quite apart from its moralistic and moralizing function, moreover, the insistence on

becoming the object of severe moral criticism is found in the oration delivered in 129 B.C. by Scipio Aemilianus who was nevertheless one of the most convinced champions of the Hellenization of Roman culture (fr.19 Malcovati). Cf.A.D.Leeman, *Orationis ratio. The Stylistic Theories and Practice of the Roman Historians and Philosophers* I, Amsterdam 1963, p.53.

35. On the fundamental pessimism of Roman historiography, see V.Pöschl, 'Die römische Auffassung der Geschichte', *Gymnasium* 63, 1956, p.190 ff.; M.Mazza, *Storia e ideologia in Tito Livio*, Catania 1965, p.78 ff.; La Penna 1967, p.187 ff.

36. B.Snell, *Antike u.Abendland* 13, 1967, p.160 ff.

37. From the narration of Arnobius 6,7 = fr.12 Peter[2] we learn that Fabius Pictor had already derived *Capitolium* from *caput Oli,* narrating the legend of the discovery of the head of Olus on the slopes of the Capitoline. Already in the work of Fabius, therefore, as in that of the later historians, this legend must have been regarded as a premonitory sign of the future destiny of Rome.

38. The categories of the beginning and the end are behind all ancient historical thought according to which that which has a beginning exists historically, while that which has no beginning is historically non-existent. On the model provided by these categories which also influence more recent cultural systems see the pages on 'cultural typology' by J.N.Lotman, *Il Verri* 2, 1973, p.25 ff. = J.N.Lotman-B.A.Uspenskij, *Tipologia della cultura*, It.trans.Milano 1975, p.135 ff.

47

the myth of the origins and the foundation of Rome is another element which can be traced back to the same school with its predilection for genealogies and for legends of the foundation of cities and their reciprocal relationships. This is an aspect which will later be accentuated in Roman historiography by Cato, who, following in this same tradition which had its most recent and authoritative interpreter in Timaeus, was to give an ethnographic slant to his historical work, placing alongside the narration of the origins of Rome an account of the origins of all the other Italic cities[39].

But also the other aspects of the polymorphic variety of "Isocratean" historiography have correspondences in the work of the first Roman historians. We see a search for narrative impulses capable of winning over the reader by means of a deliberate use of the fantastic or marvellous, for example in the recurrent and detailed description of miraculous and premonitory dreams. Some of these dreams are attributed to the legendary heroes, like the one which, according to Fabius Pictor[40], gave Aeneas a clear notion of his future exploits and of the vicissitudes he was to encounter. Others are attributed to great leaders of the more recent past, such as the dream of Hannibal narrated by Coelius Antipater[41], while yet others are ascribed to unknown and anonymous personages, entrusted by the divinity with an important message for their fellow citizens and the constitutional organs of the State[42].

The interest common to Theopompus and Timaeus in the customs of the peoples and ritual usages was undoubtedly already present in Fabius Pictor. We see this from the description of the first magnificent celebration of the Roman games[43],

39. On the influence the work of Timaeus had on Cato, enlightening remarks may be found in De Sanctis 1953, p.60 ff.; L.Moretti, 'Le Origines di Catone, Timeo ed Eratostene', Riv.filol.class. 30, 1952, p.289 ff.
40. Fr.3 Peter[2].
41. Fr.11 Peter[2].
42. Fab.Pic.fr.15 Peter[2]. According to the testimony of Cicero, De div.1,26,55, the episode of the peasant's dream recalled by Fabius Pictor also appeared in the work of other historians such as Gellius and Coelius Antipater.
43. Fr.16 Peter[2].

a type of account representing the event in a spectacular visual form so as to revive it in all its "mimetic reality" according to a narrative procedure peculiar to the so-called tragic historiography of Duris and Phylarchus.

In presenting the earliest performance of the ceremony of the games Dionysius himself[44] feels the need to state that his purpose is not so much to make the account more attractive with "spectacular" narrative tones as to provide further confirmation of the thesis of the Greek origin of the Roman people. But when he recognizes these "theatrical" aspects (προσθήκας θεατρικάς) of the narrative he is about to begin, he implies that these same characteristics were also present in Fabius, from whom he claims to have taken the description of the ceremony[45]. Such a narrative element also permeated the account on the origins, if Plutarch[46] perceived in it a conspicuously "dramatic" character common to the analogous account of Diocles of Peparethos, which Plutarch himself indicated as Fabius' source[47].

After the decisive defeat of King Antiochus III of Syria (190 B.C.), the Romans, having virtually attained the hegemony of the Mediterranean in the East as well as in the West, felt less need of a political alliance with a part of the Greek world. Little by little, therefore, that diplomatic and propagandistic impulse from which the historical work of Fabius Pictor and Cincius Alimentus had drawn its initial motivation diminished, as did the very reason which had made Greek the institutional language of Roman historiography. Cato's decision to adopt the Latin language was consequently timely: beyond the polemical context within which Cato himself undoubtedly set the innovation, making it a part of his tireless campaign in favour of Roman traditions and against the Hellenizing fashion, it responded to a truly new situation, which rendered nonsensical

44. 7,70,1.
45. 7,71,1.
46. *Rom*.8,9.
47. Aspects of tragic historiography in the work of Fabius Pictor, as well as in that of Philinus of Acragas, have been spotted by Walbank 1945, p.1 ff.

the use of Greek once the public at which historical writing was aimed had changed. The example of Cato was therefore followed unhesitantly by others, such as L. Cassius Hemina, L. Calpurnius Piso Frugi, C. Fannius and Gnaeus Gellius, who all narrated the history of Rome in Latin, beginning with the myth of the origins and ending with events they themselves had experienced.

This decline of the Greek language as the instrument of historical narrative is clearly documented by Cato's witty criticism[48] of his contemporary Aulus Postumius Albinus. The latter, faithful to the use of Greek, felt bound to display a gratuitous modesty in the proem of his work, and to excuse himself for eventual stylistic imperfections[49].

The most eloquent sign of the change of the times may be perceived in the fact that Aulus Postumius Albinus not only attracted the polemical darts of Cato, whose touchy anti-Hellenism was sometimes incompatible with an objective judgment, but was also derided for his snobbish and ingenuous Graecomania by Polybius himself[50] in an unusually humurous and vivid page of his *Histories*.

The linguistic substitution did not of course entail a different orientation in institutional principles and narrative techniques. The model of Timaeus remained in force; indeed with Cato, as we have seen, Timaeus' influence increased. At this point, rather, the need arose of applying to Latin the same principles which regulated the art of elocution in Greek historiography of the "Isocratean" school. It was certainly an arduous task which Cato was reluctant to undertake on account of his systematic rejection of stylistic research and the theory that the word should be a mere instrument of communication.

In a celebrated passage in *De oratore*[51], Cicero confirms that the first Roman historians in Latin, from Cato to L. Calpurnius

48. *Ap*.Gell.11,8,1.
49. Fr.1 Peter².
50. 39,1.
51. 2,12,53-54.

Piso Frugi, had no interest in the stylistic problem, maintaining that the only true value of the word was concision, the capacity of expressing concepts with the maximum clarity and the maximum brevity. By so doing, Cicero again observes, they were following the example of the pontifical annals. This latter affirmation has been misunderstood by those who have sought to interpret it as an unassailable proof of the substantial continuity in Roman culture between pontifical historiography and literary historiography[52]. Instead it refers exclusively to elocution, as is proved by Cicero's insistence on the lack of stylistic ornaments (*sine ullis ornamentis ... neque tenent quibus rebus ornetur oratio*).

Where the organization of historical writing is concerned, the full distance both of Piso and of Cato from the narrative technique of the Pontifices may be measured if we consider certain heavily mimetic and dramatic passages, such as Piso's description of Romulus' behaviour during the banquet, or Cato's famous passage on the voluntary sacrifice and military virtue of the tribune Q. Caedicius[53].

The first Roman author who felt the need of a formal elaboration in historical writing in Latin was Coelius Antipater, whose adherence to the historiography of the Isocratean school also emerges from the taste for the hyperbolic and the marvellous which characterizes some fragments of his monograph on the Hannibalic war[54]. He theorized about the problem of style in the proem of his work, underlining the difficulty of conciliating the rhythmic requirements of the sentence with those of a correct arrangement of the words from a linguistic point of view. Given the scantiness of the fragments we are certainly not able to formulate a judgment on the results of his stylistic commitment. In any case Cicero regarded them as significant in relation to the epoch in which Coelius Antipater had worked, but insufficient and clearly superseded by the later

52. Bömer 1953, p.195.
53. Fr.83 Peter[2].
54. Frr.11; 39 Peter[2].

historiographical production[55].

But the fundamentally Isocratean nature of the earliest Roman historiography was called in doubt by Polybius, both through the objective novelty of his work, and the harsh and violent polemic he conducted on several occasions against Timaeus and, besides Timaeus, against Ephorus and Theopompus, the two direct disciples of Isocrates. Polybius does not criticize the Roman historians directly but limits himself to demolishing the authority of the Greek masters from whom they had learned their art. Ultimately, Roman historical writing must have appeared to him as a marginal phenomenon which interested him more because of the concrete problems relating to the history of Rome than because of the methodological position.

The first to object to the method followed by the Roman historians from Fabius Pictor onwards was Sempronius Asellio, connected, like Polybius, with the cultural circle of the Scipio and who, together with Polybius, Panaetius and Lucilius, took part in Scipio Aemilianus' expedition to Numantia. Gellius[56] has transmitted some propositions of a methodological nature in the first book of his work which are the most explicit and coherent affirmation of the basic principles of the "apodeictic" method as opposed to the narrative techniques of the earlier Roman historiography:

But between those who have desired to leave us annals, and those who have tried to write the history of the Roman people (*inter eos qui annales relinquere voluissent et eos qui res gestas a Romanis perscribere conati sunt*), there was this essential difference. The books of annals merely made known what happened and in what year it happened, which is like writing a diary, which the Greeks call ἐφημερίς. For my part, I realize that it is not enough to make known what had been done, but that one should also show with what purpose and for what reasons things were done (*etiam quo consilio quoque retione gesta essent demonstrare*) [...]. For annals cannot in any way make men more eager

55. *De or.*2,12,54; *Or.*69,229; *Brut.*26,102; *De leg.*1,2,6.
56. 5,18,7-9 = frr.1-2 Peter[2].

to defend their country, or more reluctant to do wrong. Furthermore, to write over and over again in whose consulship a war was begun and ended, and who in consequence entered the city in a triumph, and in that book not to narrate what happened in the course of the war (*quae in eo bello gesta sint iterare*), without explaining what decrees the senate made during that time, or what law or bill was passed, and with what motives these things were done — that is to tell stories to children, not to write history[57] (*id fabulas pueris est narrare, non historias scribere*). [Translated by J.C. Rolfe, with some slight changes].

Two different ways of presenting a historical discourse are here contrasted; one is purely expository, orientated towards the simple statement of the facts. The other is analytic and demonstrative, intent on discovering the reasons and the intentions behind the events. The first way is defined as *annales relinquere,* the second as *res gestas perscribere.* But if the antithesis is extremely clear in itself, endless discussions have arisen about the type of historiography which Sempronius Asellio has in mind in his polemic. The difficulties spring from an interpretative hypothesis, which almost all scholars have unhesitantly adopted as obvious and unworthy of further verification, but which appears highly questionable in the light of a more attentive analysis. It was thought that the term *annales* and Sempronius' definitions of the corresponding way of writing history (*annales*

57. As we know the final part of the passage presents a textual problem to which various solutions have been given: *scribere autem, bellum initum quo consule et quo confectum sit et quis triumphans introierit ex eo libro quae in eo bello gesta sint, iterare id fabulas non praedicare aut interea quid senatus decreverit aut quae lex rogatiove lata sit neque quibus consiliis ea gesta sint iterare: id fabulas pueris est narrare, non historias scribere.* The solution here proposed is that of R.Till, which reads: *iterare, [id fabulas] non praedicare ... ea gesta sint, [iterare] id fabulas.* This textual choice was questioned by E.Pasoli in reviewing the first edition of the present volume (*Lingua e stile* 13, 1978, pp.323-325). Even if his arguments which had already appeared in critical publications do not lack substance and deserve attentive consideration, we nevertheless believe that the reasons which induced us to accept Till's hypothesis prevail. On the other hand we do not agree with him in regarding the expression *ex eo libro* (*et eo libro* Till), as an interpolation. We accept, rather, the point of view of Gabba, Timpanaro, Di Benedetto (cf.Momigliano 1966, p.59 n.9), and M.Mazza, in *Studi in memoria di C.Sgroi (1893-1952),* Torino 1965, p.575 f.

libri tantummodo quod factum quoque anno gestum sit etc.) indicated the type of narrative represented by the pontifical annals. This interpretation was to generate a series of contradictions since Sempronius' theoretical formulation seems to involve the whole preceding historical tradition and not only the pontifical annals which had just found their definitive form in the volumes of the *Annales Maximi* published around 120 B.C.

The attempts to solve the problem have proceeded in three different directions:

1) It has been supposed that post-Catonian annalistic history written in Latin in the 2nd century B.C. returned, for its narrative technique and style, to the forms of the commentaries of the Pontifices[58]. The publication of the *Annales Maximi* would thus represent the final result of that historiographical tendency. This is a very feeble hypothesis which does not find sufficient confirmation in the texts.

2) According to a different hypothesis[59], Sempronius' polemic is exclusively directed against the pontifical chronicle, contrasting its arid record of the facts with the method of literary historiography. This interpretation would be defensible if one could demonstrate that all Roman historiography from Fabius onwards was of the pragmatic-apodeictic type, and thus satisfied the methodological requirements of Sempronius. But this hypothesis, as we have seen, does not have a solid foundation.

3) Others[60] maintain that the contrast delineated by Sempronius corresponds to the one that Polybius introduces between the "genealogical" genre and the "pragmatic" genre: a distinction between a historiography of the mythical age of the origins and the foundation of cities and the historiography of political facts. The division traced by Sempronius would be "vertical, not horizontal", in the sense that, by putting all the preceding historians on the same level, he would constrast

58. Gelzer 1969, p.130 ff.
59. Gelzer 1969, p.144 ff.; Till 1949/50, p.331.
60. Bömer 1953.

within their works the first part, normally devoted to the myth of the origins, with the second, relating instead to political history. In this perspective, Sempronius condemns the purely legendary nature of the genealogical narration, and expresses instead his appreciation of the second aspect of Roman historiography, seeing in it an attempt, however crude and empirical, at writing pragmatic history: the expression *conati essent* would then refer to an only partially successful experiment.

But in the passage by Sempronius there is not so much as an implicit allusion to this presumed distinction between the "genealogical" genre and the "pragmatical" genre within a single historical work. He only distinguishes between two opposed groups of historians, those who wrote annals and those who intended to write history. The first, ultimately, wrote no more than a diary, while the second dealt with the problem of the political causes of the historical facts. It is thus a contrast between two different types of historiography which manifests itself in the specific context of this formulation, in the semantic opposition between *annales* and *res gestae* or *historiae*.

If the second category alludes to historians of the Polybian type, the polemical reference to "those who have desired to leave us annals" probably involves not only the *Annales Maximi*, or the pontifical annals, but also all those earlier and coeval Roman historians who, from a strictly Polybian point of view, had limited themselves to narrating facts without a rigorous and objective exposition of the causes. A passage like Fabius' on the causes of the second Punic war is really not of the "Polybian type": Polybius himself, as we have seen, had rejected his analysis as destitute of any foundation.

An argument which has been much emphasized in order to deny the contrast between Sempronius Asellio and the first period of Roman literary historiography is derived from a sentence of Polybius[61] in which the work of Aulus Postumius Albinus is referred to with the expression *pragmatikè historía*. But also in this case we have an erroneous interpretation:

61. 39,1,4.

pragmatikós is an adjective that Polybius uses to indicate the object, not the method, of a historiographical work. The work of Postumius Albinus was indeed "pragmatic history" in as much as its object was primarily recent and contemporary history. But no methodological praise is implied by the words of Polybius, who also recognizes the presence of "pragmatic history" in the work of historians who were very far from his own method[62]. *Pragmatikè historía* denotes the history of political and military facts, in contrast to that of genealogies, the foundations of cities, colonizations, etc. It is only concerned with the contents, not the methodology, of the historical narrative. For history that conforms to the rigorous principles of demonstrative method Polybius uses, as we have seen, the expression *apodeiktikè historía*[63].

To return to the central problem of our discussion, the hypothesis that Sempronius' criticism was aimed not so much at the pontifical annals as at Roman historiography of the 3rd and 2nd centuries B.C., finds a further confirmation in the semantic implications of the proposition: "that is to tell stories to children, not to write history". The idea of telling stories, as opposed to the notion of writing history, clearly alludes to a type of historical narrative which plays on the emotions of the listener or reader through the description of facts and situations apt to arouse marvel and astonishment; a type of historiography which must have used certain polymorphic narrative elements pertaining to usages, customs, legends, dreams, prodigies, etc., in other words those very elements which Dionysius of Halicarnassus later considered important in the historiography of the Isocratean Theopompus and which were of equal importance in Roman historiography before Sempronius.

Cicero, who dwells on several occasions on the theoretical problems of historical writing, implicitly and explicitly declares his predilection for the historiography of the Isocratean type, as

62. 9,1.
63. Cf. Chapter I, n.86.

A.D. Leeman[64] has rightly shown: in a letter to Lucceius[65] he introduces the term *fabula* to indicate a historical narrative which would involve the reader, awakening admiration, a sense of expectation, joy, sorrow, hope and fear, in other words a narrative of the monographic type, centred on the achievements and the changing fortunes of a highly significant historic personage rich in emotional tension. Cicero was referring, in this specific case, to the history of his consulate which Lucceius himself was supposed to write. The word *fabula* has a particular significance in Cicero's discussion, underlining the strictly *dramatic* character of a narrative which also involved elements of mimetic history. In this case, the word characterizes a type of narrative which is very different from that of the "annals"[66] because of the larger amount of emotionality inherent in its unitary and monographic dimension.

With the term "annals" Cicero clearly refers to the literary annals which narrated *year by year* the vicissitudes of Rome from the remotest antiquity up to the present time, a continuous structure which could only arouse the interest of the reader partly or to a small extent (*mediocriter*).

Cicero's page shows us how Sempronius' statement should be understood, for *fabula* seems to include that element of "drama" and "fiction" (δραματικὸν καὶ πλασματῶδες) that Plutarch found in Fabius' narrative[67]. But the views expressed by Cicero and Sempronius about the historiographical tradition differ in their content — a difference in the methodological positions of the two writers. Sempronius, like Polybius, perceived in his predecessors a kind of exposition and an accumulation of elements going back to that notion of narrative intended for an audience of children. Cicero, on the other hand, notes the inadequacy of annalistic writing when compared to the markedly

---

64. 'Le genre et le style historique à Rome: théorie et pratique', *Rev. ét.lat.*33, 1955, p.183 ff.
65. *Ad fam.*5,12,6.
66. *Ibid.*5,12,5.
67. *Rom.*8,9.

dramatic genre of history which he proposes in the letter to Lucceius.

But it is equally significant that Sempronius should use the word *iterare*, which in the theatrical language of archaic Latin has the specific meaning of "to narrate", with a sense of *suspense* or comicity, and in any case directly connected with the duration of the *fabula* (drama) and with the requirements peculiar to the performance[68].

If this is the value of the *fabulas pueris narrare*, the notion of usefulness in the expression of Sempronius Asellio assumes more cogency once it is inserted in the context of the by now traditional contrast between delight and utility which goes back to Thucydides and is more amply developed by Polybius. This notion was emphasized by C. Fannius who can also be considered a follower of the school of Polybius, probably one of those who, in the judgement of Sempronius, had already tried "to write history". It served an essentially political purpose, not to say a technical political purpose, very different to the moralization, dear to the "Isocratean" and to the earlier Roman historians. Recalling Polybius' principle that the historian himself must have a direct experience of political activity, Fannius observed in the first book of the *Annales*:

68. Cf., for example, Plaut.*Cas*.879; *Pseud*.387. For this meaning of the verb *iterare* in Plautus' comedy, see *Thes.ling.Lat*.VII/2, coll.547,75 ff.; 549,9 ff. Leo (1913, p.335 n.2), commenting on Sempronius' statement, called attention to the passage in Polybius (3,20,5) where the historian reprimands Chaereas and Sosylus for having narrated the events that immediately followed the taking of Saguntum in an inexact and contradictory manner: οὐ γὰρ ἱστορίας,ἀλλὰ κουρεακῆς καὶ πανδήμου λαλιᾶς ἔμοιγε δοκοῦσι τάξιν ἔχειν καὶ δύναμιν. While the comparison may apply to the contrast between 'historical' narrative and non-historical narrative, it does not affect the substance of the first term of the antithesis stated by Sempronius. The words κουρεακὴ καὶ πάνδημος λαλιά (gossip or fables worthy of barber shops and the common people) designate the baselessness and fallacy of unreliable news, a notion that appears in contradiction to the term *fabulae* in Sempronius' narrative. *Fabulae* refers not to inexact unfounded facts but to a type of narrative lacking a rational analysis of intentions and causes — an exposition which, from Sempronius' point of view, was only intended to entertain and delight a public of children.

When we are able to draw a lesson from the active life, many things that appear positive for the moment turn out to be negative, and many others turn out to be very different from what they seemed[69].

To identify the various currents of Roman historiography, we must return to the testimony of the ancients, but it is equally necessary to evaluate each testimony in the context of the theoretical attitude and the cultural orientation of each single author.

If some critics have been deceived by the judgement of Cicero, who places on the same level the pontifical annals and the Latin historians before Coelius Antipater, this was because they did not adequately consider the semantic context in which Cicero's affirmation occurs: here he refers only to the elocution, the "ornaments" of the style, not to the methodological groundwork of the writing. The best confirmation of the necessity of interpreting each testimony in relation to its context is offered by another verdict of Cicero's[70] concerning that same Sempronius who, as a follower of Polybius, must have displayed a lack of stylistic commitment not inferior to Cato's: Sempronius could in no way have profited from the teaching of Coelius Antipater, and fell back on the "insipid debility of the ancients" (*ad antiquorum languorem et inscitiam*). At first sight this is a surprising classification which, on the one hand, covers the Roman historiographical tradition up to Sempronius Asellio and, on the other, assesses the attempt at innovation by Coelius Antipater. But all becomes clear if we consider that Cicero is not an admirer of Polybius and that in this specific case he is concerned not with the structure of historical narrative, but with the problem of elocution in general.

So archaic Roman historiography concludes with the clear contrast between the tendency represented by Sempronius Asellio, the heir and polemical champion of the method of Polybius, and the direction pursued by Coelius Antipater who perfects the "Isocratism" of those who had preceded him, ap-

69. Fr.1 Peter[2].
70. *De leg.*1,2,6.

plying to Latin the technique elaborated by the rhetorical tradition of the Greeks. We have no explicit evidence that Coelius Antipater had adopted the doctrine of Tauriscus, according to which the object of historical investigation is a "forest without method"[71], a vast repertory of information and heterogeneous facts not susceptible to an analysis governed by rigid methodological norms. But it is certainly significant that his most illustrious disciple, the orator L. Licinius Crassus, transferred this theory from the field of historical criticism to that of rhetoric[72]. According to Cicero[73] he defended the view that, while a technique of elocution is possible for the orator since the language can be regulated by precise norms, the contents of the speech, in their inexhaustible variety and thematic diversity, cannot become the object of a schematic knowledge, but are a *silva magna*: the choice, the structure and the organization of the contents are exclusively entrusted to the discernment, the culture, and the good taste of whoever pronounces the speech.

71. Cf. p.23 n.50.
72. G.Cerri, 'Crasso, Taurisco e la selva senza metodo', *Parola d.passato* 146, 1972, pp.312-320.
73. *De or*.3,24,93.

CHAPTER III

THE IDEA OF BIOGRAPHY

At the beginning of his admirable work on the development of Greek biography, Arnaldo Momigliano (1974)[1] states peremptorily that the ancient Greeks clearly distinguished and separated biography from history. He writes (p.8 [6 of the English edition]):

> Nobody nowadays is likely to doubt that biography is some kind of history. We may well turn back to the inventors of biography, the ancient Greeks, to ask why they never recognized that biography is history.

Such a categorical affirmation immediately suggests to the reader that the present tendency to identify biography with history *tout court* is a phenomenon typical of our time and totally extraneous to Greek thought. In reality, however, as he goes on Momigliano does not always seem so convinced of what he explicitly announced as his point of departure and arrival, since he admits, with H. Homeyer[2], that Herodotus already devoted ample space within his history to biographical profiles in the fifth century (p.14 [12]). With regard to the *Philippica* of Theopompus he rightly observes "the interplay of biography and history" in a single tale (p.65 [62]). Similar observations

1. In view of the bibliographical supplements made by the author himself and the addition of a lecture not contained in the English edition (*The Development of Greek Biography*, Cambridge Mass.1971), the Italian version (by G.Donini, 1974) should be considered in every way a new edition. Gallo 1974 wrote a balanced and lucid review of the edition in English, with personal contributions of his own.
2. *Philologus* 106, 1962, p.75 ff.

appear in the pages he devotes to Xenophon and the historians of Alexander (p.52 ff. [50 ff.]). But, at this point, it is surprising to read (p.108 f. [102 f.]):

Xenophon wrote portraits of generals in the *Anabasis*. Theopompus recognized the importance of the individual as such and put one man at the centre of his historical narration in the *Philippica*. The historians of Alexander the Great followed his example. *But biography and history did not merge* [the italics are ours].

As we see, the initial idea of a clear separation between biography and history is again affirmed, in spite of the series of examples to the contrary which Momigliano himself has lucidly analysed[3].

Momigliano has had the undoubted merit of posing the problem of the relationship between biography and history in Greek culture. But in order to reach an unambiguous view we must first recognize that the two notions are intimately connected to two different conceptions of history: on the one hand history understood as a series of political events alone, on the other history seen as an anthropology that embraces all aspects of human life: selective history or global history. This diversity of approach to history, as Momigliano points out in his introductory pages, underlies the contemporary debate; but, we must add, it was also operative in the historiographic thought of the Greeks[4]. We must keep this in mind since the evaluations of biography in Greek culture, whether or not it was a kind of history, were actually connected to the very concept of history.

3. This is the main idea of the whole volume and is constantly repeated. See for ex. p.14[12]: "Biography was never considered as history in the classical world"; p.42[41]: "Indeed the implicit separation between biography and history of the fifth and fourth centuries B.C. was to become explicit later, at least from Polybius onwards"; p.117: "The distinction between biography and history (i.e. political history) was formulated as a theory in the Hellenistic period, but it already existed in practice in the 5th century ... we must acknowledge that the dichotomy between biography and history is as old as Greek historiography itself".
4. See Chapter I.

When Dionysius of Halicarnassus[5] delineates the aspects and the tendencies of the historiography of Theopompus[6], he explicitly underlines the fact that the biographical objective was one of the guiding lines of his *Histories*. In contrast to other historians, he did not make the biographical narrative (*bíos*) a sort of incidental digression (*párergon*) from the proper historical narrative, but a necessary and indispensable part of it. The foundations of cities, the lives of kings, psychological characterizations and descriptions of environments and customs, all represented what Dionysius calls the narrative *polymorphía* of the historian.

In Theopompus then the biographical interest was inseparable from the critical exposition of the facts and their causes. Dionysius writes[7]:

The most characteristic element of his historiography, which is not developed with equal care and effectiveness in any of the other historians either past or present ... is not only to see and to say what is evident to everyone in various political events, but also to seek *the hidden motives (aitíai) of the actions and of the man who accomplished them and the passions which move the soul,* which are not easy to discern in the majority of men, and to unveil the secrets of an apparent virtue and of a vice concealed and ignored.

Hence the charge of slander and acrimony (*pikría*) which Polybius levels at Theopompus, a view which marks the difference between two concepts of history attributing a different space and a different function to the use of biography[8]. It is obvious that from the point of view of the apodeictic method[9] followed by Polybius an accentuated biographism, which had a specific role of moral and psychological analysis of the events

5. *Epist.ad Pomp*.6 (II p.244 ff. Us.-Rad.) = *F.Gr.Hist*.115 T 20. See Chapter I, p.16 f.
6. Cf.p.16 f.
7. *Epist.ad Pomp*.6,7 (II p.246,6 Us.-Rad.).
8. Cfr.D.Musti, *Società antica. Antologia di storici greci,* Roma-Bari 1973, p.161.
9. On the term *apodeiktikós*, used by Polybius as the correct attribute for describing his own historical method, see p.32 n.86.

in Theopompus' global historiography, would appear mystifying in comparison with a rigorous and scientific analysis of purely political reasons.

Dionysius of Halicarnassus shows that he does not share this critical position when he observes in the *Roman Antiquities*[10] that the duty of the historian is to relate not only the military exploits of illustrious leaders or the most salutary governmental measures they have taken for the advantage of the cities, but also their private lives, emphasizing their personality and their coherence with patriotic traditions. This is a use of history in the line of Isocratean historiography, and in clear opposition to a uniform and monochord (*monoeidés*)[11] type of history, exclusively centred on political and military facts. As has been observed[12], there is an implicit polemical reference to the pragmatic history of Polybius.

Cicero proves himself to be in this same tradition in the letter to Lucceius[13]: here he elaborates on a type of history in which the monographic and unitary dimension of the narrative concentrates the reader's attention on a single personage placed at the centre of the events. As we see, this presupposes a close interaction between history and biography[14].

At this point we may wonder what the true position assumed by the theorist of pragmatic-apodeictic history was. Momigliano writes[15]:

The old and honoured distinction between history and biography — which Polybius (10, 21 [24]) had proclaimed, Plutarch (*Alex.* 1,2) had recognized, and Eduard Meyer had reconfirmed as late as 1902 — was apparently being denied by the boisterous international clan to which Emil Ludwig, André Maurois, and Lytton Strachey most conspicuously belonged.

10. 5,48,1.
11. *Ant.Rom.*1,8,1-3.
12. S.Gozzoli, 'Polibio e Dionigi di Alicarnasso', *Studi classici e orientali.* 25, 1976, p.157 f.
13. See above, p.56 f.
14. As Momigliano 1974 himself seems to acknowledge on pp.86 [83] and 124.
15. 1974, p.3[1].

But did Polybius really proclaim this "old and honoured distinction", in other words, a rigid separation of tasks and functions between historical and biographical investigation? From an objective reading it would not appear that Polybius had intended to radicalize the theoretical distinction between the two genres. Rather, he defined those elements of biographical information which could be of use within the limits of his historical method. In the chapter in question (10,21), preparing himself to deal with Philopoemen's political and military action, he observes that it would be as well to introduce a portrait of the man, illuminating above all his educational training (*agōgḗ*) and the characteristics of his temperament (*phýsis*) — a procedure which he followed where other men worthy of particular interest were concerned[16]. In his view it is only right that the formative period of the protagonists of events should be dealt with on account of its relevance and usefulness for the listeners and readers. But in this specific case Polybius abandons these biographical aspects because he has already spoken of them in a work in three books dedicated to Philopoemen in which he narrates the events of his life. Some he describes in detail (those of his private life beginning with his youth). Others are reduced to significant moments (*kephalaiōdôs*) relevant to his political activity at the climax of his career. For the purpose of his narrative he therefore has to make a choice, to give in more detail those biographical data which have a more limited space in the preceding work because of its *encomiastic* intent. What Polybius rejects is not the biographical fact or biography in general, which he instead regards as relevant, not to say essential, to the historical narrative, but an encomiastic bias proper only to a monograph destined to extol a man[17]. History, on the other hand, also on the level of biographical recognition, calls for a veracious exposition of the apodeictic type that

16. Thus, for example, about Xanthippus (1,32,1), Tarquin the Elder (6,2a,7), Hannibal (9,22), Scipio (10,2 f.), Chaeron (24,7,1). Cf.Osley 1946, p.19; P.Pédech, *Rev.ét.gr.*64, 1951, p.91.
17. Hence opposition between encomium and history, not between biography and history. Cf. the perceptive remarks by Walbank 1967, p.223.

mingles praise with blame, without neglecting any reflection or hypothesis useful for the objective, non-tendentious evaluation of the facts.

A reviewer of Momigliano's work spoke of the "divorce between political-military history and the antiquarian treatise", a divorce embracing "the entire range of antiquity" and confirmed by Polybius, both in the passage just examined and in three chapters of Book VIII[18]. Polybius affirms that the accounts of the historians of Philip of Macedon do not have the characteristics of a "history", but of an "encomium". In his view one should neither insult with lies nor flatter monarchs, but construct a narrative suitable for illustrating the principles and the choices which inspired their action. Here begins the polemic against Theopompus who, though recognizing the great merits and the genius of Philip of Macedon in his *Histories*, had insisted bitterly and violently on his intemperance and vices, using false information. Polybius really insists in both passages on the idea that the task of the historian is to evaluate objectively the vices and the virtues that animated and determined the political action, rejecting both a narrative of the encomiastic type, more pertinent to the strictly biographical account, and a tendentious and denigratory sort of narrative. Merits and demerits should be evaluated in as much as they are useful for explaining the causes of the events. What really distinguishes biography from history is the selection of the biographical data, in the first case mainly orientated towards the reconstruction of the educational development, in the second towards the cause of political and military events. There is really no dichotomy, no divorce, in Polybius, between historical and biographical narrative, only a fortunate interaction between the two, with a different accentuation on the one or the other according to the type of work written.

In the field of the biographical essay, on the other hand, Plutarch interprets this same need to select the material in order

18. 8 (10) - 10 (12). We refer to the essay by G.Camassa, *Quaderni d.storia* 4, 1976, p.249 ff.

to limit the area of interference between the two fields of interest, with a special view to his own particular type of writing. Addressing his readers in the introduction to the *Life of Nicias* he says that he will deal briefly with those same actions and events which have already been treated so expertly by previous historians like Thucydides and Philistus, events and actions that nevertheless implicate the nature and the behaviour of the characters. He will refer summarily to them for the sake of completeness, but will try to concentrate on those events which have been ignored by many writers and are attested by epigraphic documents and decrees. His object is not so much to compile a useless history (*historía*), but to offer the reader the material necessary for understanding the nature and the behaviour of the protagonist. He shows a full awareness of the different approach of the two types of narrative according to the different functions of the biographer and the historian. This is the sense in which we should also take the peremptory statement contained in the introduction to the *Life of Alexander*: "For it is not Histories I am writing but Lives; not only in the most illustrious deeds is there a manifestation of virtue or vice, nay, a slight thing like a phrase or a jest often makes a greater revelation of character than battles where thousands fall, or the greatest armaments, or sieges of cities"[19].

The theoretical premise is that of Polybius, but reversed, as it were, to suit the focus of the biographer, even if the awareness of the complex mediations between the two distinct and complementary levels of writing remains.

With regard to the relationship between history and biography in the thought and the works of Plutarch, we cannot but refer to the illuminating pages by Mazzarino, who has centred the problem. About *Alex.* 1, he writes[20]: "Here there is indeed a rejection of *history* as a literary genre of extended narration; but not the rejection of historical investigation and the historical

19. Cf.also *Galb.*2,3.
20. 1966, II/2 p.137.

art as such, even if it be concentrated on the form of life of the various personalities, that is, on the *ethos*"[21].

When faced with this problem, what is the point of associating biography with erudition and antiquarianism, in an arbitrary simplification, which opposes it to political-military history? The simplification confers the dignity of history only on the selective narration of political and military facts, i.e. exclusively on Thucydidean and Polybian history. Thus not only biography, but also the global Isocratean or mimetic historiography fall back into the cauldron of erudition, while the former was of an anthropological nature and the latter was essentially dramatic[22].

On the other hand, the frequently repeated distinction[23] between a biography of an erudite nature and a biography with a more complex structure, including historical, political, ideological and ethical elements, would not be understood in a schematic sense, but in relation to the function and to the type of audience for which the individual biographical narrative is intended[24]. In his recent volume on Suetonius[25] H. Gugel starts with this need to surpass certain schematic classifications which tend to flatten the multiple reality of biographical narrative. His criticism stems from a concrete analysis of the *Lives of the Caesars,* which can hardly be reduced to the idea, elaborated by Leo, of a biography of an erudite nature and of grammatical derivation[26]. A correct analysis of Greek biography should thus

21. For the interpretation of the two programmatic passages, and to the manner in which Plutarch used his sources, see now B.Scardigli, *Die Römer-biographien Plutarchs,* München 1979, p.3 ff.

22. We have clearly individuated the various tendencies of Greek historiography in Chapter I. Camassa misrepresents the thought of Momigliano whose work is substantially alien to formalistic classifications, as Gallo (1974, p.186) has rightly remarked.

23. Leo 1901.

24. On the notion of allocutory activity in relation to the theory of genres, see E.W.Bruss, 'L'autobiographie considerée comme acte littéraire', *Poétique* 17, 1974, p.16, with bibliography (French translation by J.-P.Richard).

25. *Studien zur biographischen Technik Suetons,* Wien-Köln-Graz 1977.

26. The opposition he established somewhat mechanically between a "Suetonian" and a "Plutarchean" type of biography was recently attacked

proceed from within, that is, from the identification of the purpose the author has set himself. This principle reveals its validity for examples with regard to the cultural system of the 6th and 5th cent. B.C., when we consider the various motivations behind the Homeric biography of Theagenes and the biographical pages in Herodotus' history.

The object of Theagenes, a rhapsode of the second half of the 6th century B.C., was evidently to furnish the audience of his public recitals of Homeric poems with some essential information on the activity, the family and the epoch of the poet whose verses he recited[27] — a custom observed in a later epoch by other interpreters of Homer like Stesimbrotus of Thasos and Antimachus of Colophon. Different, instead, was the function and, consequently, the typology of the biographical insertion intimately connected with the historical context in Herodotus. Different, too, was the point of view adopted by Ion of Chios for the gallery of biographical portraits in the work (*Epidēmíai*) in which he narrated his meetings at Chios or in other Greek cities with intellectuals and politicians of his time[28]. It is a series of *close-ups* — to use the title of a recent work by Domenico Porzio devoted to interviews with contemporaries — which describe the typical behaviour of the protagonists at significant moments of their daily life. Episodes such as the one when Sophocles contrives a stratagem during a banquet in order to attract the boy who is serving wine and kiss him are neither banal nor gratuitous, but illustrate human qualities, like lasciviousness and wit, in the personality of a great poet who, Ion adds, was only a mediocre politician[29]. Between the lines we sense a

also by I.Gallo on the basis of new material furnished by the discovery of papyri (*Frammenti biografici da papiri*, II: *La biografia dei filosofi*, Roma 1980, p.18).

27. Fr.8 B 1 D.-K., cf.Pfeiffer 1968, p.11.

28. *F.Gr.Hist.*392 F 4 ff. Judging from their content, some fragments of Ion transmitted by the sources without any indication of the work from which they were taken and inserted by Jacoby in the section of fragments with no title, undoubtedly belong to the *Epidēmíai*. In the following brief discussion we have used them in order to reconstruct Ion's technique of portraiture.

29. F 6.

subtle psychological observation which holds true to this day: intellectuality and the exercise of power are not easily reconcilable virtues. The psychological biographical purpose of such anecdotes is also discernible in the encounter with Cimon at a symposium: unlike Sophocles he is not thinking of love but of music. He demonstrates his singing ability and then narrates his stratagem for deceiving the allies in the division of the spoils of war[30]. His behaviour is consistent with Ion's overall judgement of the man, insisting on his tact, on his shrewdness, and on the jovial urbanity of his social behaviour[31].

Similarly, attitudes of arrogance, superiority, disdain and contempt for others are detected in the personality of Pericles — attitudes in striking contrast with the amability and sociability of Cimon. These aspects of his character are certainly reprehensible, but Ion justified them by affirming that human virtue always has something unseemly and laughable as an intrinsic element, just as a tragic performance always has its satirical moment[32].

In Ion of Chios we undoubtedly already find the basis of a portrait which represents the entirety of a man's character, his positive and his negative qualities[33]. It is a biographical technique which does not even neglect particular physical features, as in the case of Cimon, tall in stature, impeccable in appearance, with thick curly hair[34].

It has been rightly said that the biographical portrait differs from the figurative portrait because it introduces "duration and movement"[35] — movement in the sense of existential vicissitudes. This is an aspect that the figurative portrait can in no way describe, while it can, on the other hand, represent the movement of the man in action. We have only to recall the group of tyrannicides, sculpted by Kritios and Nesiotes for the

30. F 13.
31. Plut. *Per.*5,3 = F 15.
32. F 15.
33. Hölscher (1973, p.209 f.) has rightly noted this.
34. F 12.
35. J.Starobinski, 'Le style de l'autobiographie', *Poétique* 3, 1970, p.257.

agorá of Athens, in which Harmodius and Aristogiton are represented in the positive moment of the combative action, not in the negative moment of their death[36]. Both, however, presuppose the same cultural context in which interest centres on the realistic representation and comprehension of the ethos of illustrious men. Nor can we speak of biographical narrative and neglect the phenomenon of the portrait in the figurative arts, a relationship which has been detected by historians and art historians more than by literary historians[37]. It is hardly a coincidence that it should be in the artistic milieu of Chios that we have some of the first portraits, like the gem of Boston, with the physiognomic portrait of a bearded man carved by Dexamenos between 450 and 430 B.C.[38], in the very years when Ion was probably composing the *Epidēmíai*. We can safely go still further and note that the portrait of Pericles by Kresilas really represented that combination, emphasized by Ion, of severe nobility and *satyrikón* in Pericles' temperament. It is rendered by the realistic treatment of the elongated form of the skull, "squill-head"[39], which was, as Plutarch observes[40], subject to recurrent attacks by the comic poets. There are, moreover, attestations of physiognomic portraits, some decades earlier, like, for example, the one by the painter Egesibulus, portraying an old Jew leaning on a cane and accompanied by his dog[41]. Nor

36. See I.Calabi Limentani, *Acme* 29, 1976, p.15.

37. We refer especially to the book by Hölscher (1973) and the intelligent observations of Finley 1976, p.86.

38. Cf.Erika Diehl, 'Eine Gemme des Dexamenos', *Berliner Museen* 16, 1966, p.44 ff., fig.2; D.Metzler, *Porträt und Gesellschaft*, Münster 1971, p.309, fig.25. The relationship we have mentioned between the figurative portrait and the literary portrait was the subject of a seminar held in May 1977 at the Institute of Classical Philology, Urbino, by C.Gasparri, to whom our thanks are due.

39. Cf.B.Schweitzer, 'Bedeutung und Geburt des Porträts bei den Griechen', *Acta Congressus Madvigiani* 3, 1957, p.35 ff. = *Zur Kunst der Antike. Ausgewählte Schriften* II, Tübingen 1963, p.196 ff. Metzler's scepticism seems excessive, *op.cit.*p.217 ff., when he maintains that the detail of visible locks of hair in the eye openings in the helmet is a mere "artistic motif".

40. *Per.*3,4-7.

41. J.Boardman, *Athenian Redfigure Vases. The Archaic Period,* London 1975, p.62 and fig.126.

should we overlook the important information in Plutarch[42] on the poet Simonides, mocked by Themistocles for his mania of having his portrait done in spite of his ugliness. This presupposes that the need for a degree of similarity between the portrait and the physical features of the subject was already felt in that period.

Certainly, the portraits sketched by Ion in the *Epidēmíai* recall the technique of the painted portrait more than a real biographical narrative. As far as we can tell from the available fragments, however, they must have contained one of the distinctive elements of later biography, concentrating on daily behaviour rather than on the great historic events, on a significant daily routine in which the *ethos* of the hero is thoroughly displayed.

Biographical impulses can, of course, be discerned even in a work like the *Certamen between Homer and Hesiod*, which may probably be attributed to the Sophist Alcidamas[43]. Here the two poets are presented practising their profession, in a reconstruction that certainly borrowed elements from the rhapsodic tradition which, as we noted in the case of Theagenes, combined the exposition of biographical information about the poet with the declamation of Homeric poems. In this specific case the information comes from an autobiographical reference by Hesiod himself[44] which recounts a poetic agon in which he took part in the city of Chalkis. The reference may be qualified as the earliest allusion to autobiography, and it clearly situates the poet in a context typical of oral culture and rhapsodic agonism. In this relationship between the biography and the poetic work, we have the first signs of the method which G. Kaibel perceived in Aristotle's *Constitution of Athens* where the section referring to the life and work of Solon is illustrated and documented with

42. *Them.*5,7.
43. For the attribution to Alcidamas and an analysis of the narrative technique perceptible in the composition, cf.E.Vogt, *Rh.Mus.*102, 1959, p.193 ff.; Arrighetti 1977, p.23 ff.
44. *Op.*654 ff.

the poet's verses. This narrative scheme becomes the rule in the lives of the lyric poets by the Aristotelian Chamaeleon and in the *Life of Euripides* by Satirus[45]. An identical technique seems to be used in a treatise on the lyric poets (Alcman, Stesichorus, Sappho, Alcaeus)[46], particularly in the most legible part of the papyrus which concerns Alcaeus. With reference to the accusation made against the poet by a boy, Amardis, of having killed a man (probably Pittacus), the poem is quoted in which Alcaeus expressly proclaims his innocence ("I am in no way guilty of the blood ... ")[47], attributing responsibility for the deed to one of the Allienes. This expository method suggests a Peripatetic ancestry, confirmed by the explicit quotation of Aristotle, Dicaearchus and Chamaeleon.

At this point one may wonder why Aristotle and his school rigorously stuck to this type of biographical narrative interwoven with poetic quotations. The answer lies in the pragmatic nature of all archaic lyric poetry and in the recurrent autobiographical elements which the poet inserted in his work either for propagandistic and apologetic purposes or in relation to the daily vicissitudes of his private life. This kind of poetry was the most immediate point of reference for the biographer who had to evaluate the information provided in the text on the basis of other evidence, taking into consideration the necessarily personal and subjective perspective of the poet oscillating between truth and fiction. This procedure was naturally undermined by the tendency not always to distinguish with proper attention between the *I* of the *persona loquens* and the *I* of the author.

In this respect we must emphasize the complete scepticism

---

45. See Arrighetti 1977. On some errors in the biographies of Euripides caused by the tendency to accept literally the metaphors and critical allegories elaborated at the expense of the poet by the "hyper-real world" of the ancient Attic comedy, see P.Fornaro, 'Γένος Εὐριπίδου: commedia e biografia', *Vichiana* 8, 1979, p.3 ff.

46. *P.Oxy.*2506, ed.D.Page, *The Oxyrhynchus Papyri* XXIX, 1963; cf. M.Treu, *Quad.Urb.*2, 1966, p.9 ff.; *R.E.* Supplbd.XI, s.v.'Sappho', col.1228 f.

47. *P.Oxy.*2506, fr.77,20 ff. = fr.306 A b Voigt.

displayed in the last few years by certain groups of critics inclined to treat the references to real life and to contemporary reality
in archaic lyrical poetry as purely literary inventions[48]. Poetry,
by its nature, undoubtedly organizes referential reality in an
autonomous linguistic universe. Consequently it would be absurd to reduce it to a mere chronicle. But it is equally erroneous
to consider poetic reality as completely free of any historical
reference, as if we were always dealing with a system of conventional inventions. Yet this is the implicit assumption of whoever
denies the pragmatic aspects of archaic Greek poetry deriving
from its specific function in relation to the audience and the
concrete situation. Instead, in each case we must distinguish the
various levels of reality used by the poet. Let us take the poetry
of Archilochus, which really was a poetry of daily life with its
autobiographical dimension. It deals, in a concrete and direct
manner, with his relations with the community of his fellow-
citizens in the alternating episodes of political struggle and col-
onial ventures on the isle of Thasos. It is a poetry permeated
with historical data, political polemics and all the characteristic
motifs of the serio-comic, from personal attack to the playful
and farcical representation of persons and situations. This vision of the poetry of Archilochus, moreover, is confirmed by a
fairly straightforward biographical tradition of which Critias,
the Athenian intellectual and politician of the late 5th century
B.C., is our oldest representative[49]: he speaks of having derived
from the verses of the poet information about the emigration
from Paros to Thasos and the political events which determined
it. And, beyond the biographical tradition, the early historiography of Paros and Thasos, as we know, did not hesitate to use
the poetry of Archilochus as a primary and direct source. The
particular structure of poetry, though sometimes containing
polemical or even mystifying messages, is not a reason for deny-

48. Typical of this attitude is the essay of M.R.Lefkowitz, 'The Poet as
Hero: Fifth-Century Autobiography and Subsequent Biographical Fiction',
Class.Quart.28, 1978, pp.459-469.
49. Fr.88 B 44 D.-K. = Archil.Test.46 Tarditi.

ing its relationship with the historic event. In the case of Archilochus the information which can be inferred from his poetry corresponds perfectly to the evidence furnished by archaeological research[50].

On the whole, any autobiographical narrative is the account of a "human action"[51], if it is true that the essence of man is the combination of the social contacts in which he lives. Autobiography, therefore, always implies a process of construction and reconstruction of the social element, in the sense that the individual "takes it over, mediates it, filters it and retranslates it projecting it in another dimension, which is the dimension of his subjectivity"[52].

Also in the tradition of the serio-comic poetry of Archilochus we have a significant autobiographical document in which a poet of Thasos, Hegemon (5th century B.C.), narrates in hexameters his personal and professional experiences, recalling the success achieved in Athens in the rhapsodic agons and the abundant earnings obtained[53]. The great favour that he encountered in the Athenian public with his epico-rhapsodic recitals is confirmed by the biographer Chamaeleon[54] with regard to his memorable performance of the parodic narrative of the *Gigantomachia*, which provoked an uncontrollable outburst of laughter in the audience.

But apart from the personal references to the poets' own live with which archaic poetry is interlaced, autobiography had its effect on historiographical production in the ancient world more as a propagandistic and apologetic narrative intended to specify contingent facts and socio-political situations than as the

50. Cf.J.Pouilloux, in *Archiloque, Entret.Hardt* X, Vandoeuvres-Genève 1963, p.3 ff. and B.Gentili, *Poesia e pubblico nella Grecia antica*, Roma-Bari 1984, p.233 ff.

51. F.Ferrarotti, *Storia e storie di vita*, Roma-Bari 1981, p.41.

52. F.Ferrarotti, *op.cit.*p.42.

53. Cf.P.Brandt, *Parodorum Epicorum Graecorum et Archestrati Reliquiae*, Lipsiae 1888, p.42, = *Poeti parodici greci* a cura di E.Degani, Bologna 1982, p.39 ff.

54. Fr.43 Steffen = 44 Wehrli.

deliberate choice of a literary genre. It is in this sense that we should understand the view of Wilamowitz and Leo[55], who denied to ancient culture the idea of autobiography understood as a reconstruction of one's own existential development represented in the multiplicity of one's moral and intellectual experiences[56]. On the other hand, if we give to the term *autobiography* the general meaning of "biography of one's self", that is, of a type of narrative which requires the identification of the narrator with the protagonist of the facts narrated, we have to admit that autobiography was not unknown to the Greeks. But what was at stake was a type of narrative intended to furnish *memorabilia* and direct testimonies of diplomatic, military and political facts which could later be used in a real historical narrative: hence the significantly reductive title of "notes", "memories" (*hypomnémata, commentarii*). This is the function Cicero[57] attributes to the *Commentarii* of Caesar, when, acknowledging the beauty and the plainness of the writing, he observes that, composed by the author in order to offer the necessary documentation to the historian, they really dissuade anyone with any discernment from reelaborating a work already perfect in its genre.

It is therefore evident that the vast work of Misch (1950) on the history of ancient autobiography, though still containing the most exhaustive research on the subject, is marred by the preliminary definition of autobiography as "history of human self-awareness". As Momigliano [58] has rightly observed, this definition, influenced by W. Dilthey, does not really apply to ancient texts since true autobiography in the modern sense which associates self-awareness with the narration of facts only

55. U.von Wilamowitz, *Intern. Wochenschrift für Wissenschaft. Kunst und Technik* 1, 1907, p.1105; Leo 1913, p.342.

56. Leo's position is specified by E.Fraenkel in a letter to Momigliano of 24 February 1968 and now published by the latter in his book (1974, p.102 n.23): Leo's attitude is not due to ignorance or neglect of a whole series of autobiographical writings by Greek authors, but to the fact that he maintains "too distinct" a division in literary genres.

57. *Brutus* 75, 262.

58. 1974, p.20 [17 f.].

begins with the *Confessions* of St. Augustine. Thus, J. Starobinski, having pointed out "the importance of the personal experience, the necessity of offering a sincere account to others", adds[59]:

> This presupposition establishes the legitimacy of the *I* and authorizes the subject of the narrative to take his past existence as a theme. Moreover the *I* is confirmed in its function as permanent subject by the presence of its correlative *you* that confers its motivation on the narrative. I am thinking of the *Confessions* of St. Augustine: the author addresses God with the intention of edifying his readers.

The very term *autobiography* was not invented until the 19th century and it is in the last two centuries that this type of narrative has become institutionalized as a literary activity endowed with a certain margin of autonomy. Contrary to what happened in ancient memoirs, psycho-affective revelation has become obligatory in the eyes of the modern reader: its omission would be felt as an absence of information. The verifiability of the facts plays a secondary role in respect to "sincerity"[60].

To conclude, ancient autobiography was a narrative genre whose "generic" *dominant* feature[61], apart from some sporadic hints at anecdotes from daily life (as, for example, in the *Hypomnémata* of Ptolemy VIII Evergetes II)[62], was its apologetic and propagandistic objective. This objective assumes a completely explicit character in the *Bios* of Flavius Josephus, the most ancient autobiography which has come down to us in

59. *Art.cit.*p.260. See also E.Vance ('Le moi comme langage', *Poétique* 14, 1973, p.163 ff.), who, however, strongly emphasizes the difference between romantic autobiography and the "mnemonic *epistémē*" peculiar to St. Augustine, that is, his aptitude for seeking divine truth, in the memory of his own past.

60. E.W.Bruss, *art.cit.*p.26. On the impossibility of a metahistorical definition of the concept of autobiography, see Ph.Lejeune, 'Le pacte autobiographique', *Poétique* 14, 1973, p.137 ff.

61. The notion of "dominant feature ", used by the Russian formalists in relation to the theory of genres, seems relevant here: see, for example, J.Tynjanov, 'Il fatto letterario', in *Avanguardia e tradizione*, It.trans. by S.Leone, Bari 1968, p.23 ff.

62. *F.Gr.Hist.*234.

its original form: here, after a brief introductory note on the family from which he came and on his education, the narration of the historic events of which the author had been a protagonist begins in the third chapter. The declared purpose of the book is to reveal the author's attitude in one of the most critical moments of the history of his people, i.e. at the moment when the conflict exploded between the Jews and the Romans. It is nothing less than a self-defence against the accusations and insinuations of his political adversaries. Similarly *His Own Life* by Nicolaus of Damascus[63] would be an apologetic self-portrait, at times striking the unusual note of the self-encomium, if we did not entertain serious doubts about whether the writings *De virtutibus* and *De periculis* really contain authentic extracts from his work[64].

The treatise on his own books by the doctor-philosopher Galen of Pergamum, who lives in the 2nd century A.D., is an exception[65]. It is a curious work, destined to become, from late antiquity until modern times, a model for the autobiography of an intellectual or a scientist. It hardly assumes the form of a true autobiography since it is primarily a review of the medical texts composed by the author in the course of his professional activity. However, in the relationship constantly maintained between every book and the events that determined its composition, the itinerary of Galen's cultural formation in his youth and his pro-

---

63. *F.Gr.Hist.*90 F 131-139.

64. It is hardly credible, particularly if we keep fr. 137 in mind, that this is the original text of Nicolaus' autobiography, as Misch (1950, p.307 f.), Jacoby (II C, p.288 f.) and most recently Momigliano (1974, p.92 f.[91]) maintain. The difficulty is constituted not so much by the use of the third person, which has an obvious parallel in the *Commentarii* of Caesar and in the *De memoria vitae suae* of Augustus, of whom Nicolaus himself wrote a biography (*F.Gr.Hist.*90 F 125-130; cf. B.Scardigli, *Studi it.filol.class.*50, 1978, pp.245-252), as by the eulogy, which Leo already regarded as "singular" for an autobiography (1901, p.191 n.3). The most probable hypothesis, already advanced by 19th century philology, is that the present text is the work of a fervent admirer who used Nicolaus' autobiography.

65. *Galeni scripta minora* II, pp.91-124 (Περὶ τῶν ἰδίων βιβλίων) Mueller; cf.Galeno, *Opere scelte*, ed.I Garofalo and M.Vegetti, Torino 1978, pp.61-90.

gressive, inspiring conquest of medical sciences is recounted with precise self-awareness. The existential development is seized in the decisive moment of an intellectual experience strongly attuned to the search for knowledge and wisdom rather than in the external events of his life.

This type of reflection on one's own studies and education still survives: take, for example, the classic work of Sigmund Freud, *My Life and Psychoanalysis (Selbstdarstellung)* and, more recently, K. Popper's book[66], in which the author tries to offer a panorama of the ideas and problems on which he has worked in recent years and which are still the object of his research. It is an autobiography in which historical facts, encounters with eminent personalities or episodes in the author's daily life are indeed mentioned when they have some connection with the development of his theories. Thus, in the autobiography of the physicist Max Born the itinerary of his scientific research, from his early youth up to his mature years spent in voluntary exile, is interwoven with such tragic events as the persecution of the Jews and, later, the Second World War. It is a peaceful, relaxed narrative, which is nevertheless animated by the passion of the scientist and a constant concern with the future of European culture[67].

Galen has shown that we can speak of our books as a vital experience; but it is equally true that the story of our life may be traced through the books not written but read by us, as Henry Miller shows — his is a kind of examination of conscience conducted through the reevocation and critical analysis of books read by choice or by chance[68].

Studies on ancient biography and autobiography, and on other literary genres, have been almost exclusively concerned with problems of a genetic type, often approached too schematically and accompanied by ideas and categories more

66. *Unended Quest: an Intellectual Autobiography*, London 1976.
67. M.Born, *My Life. Recollections of a Nobel Laureate*, London-New York 1978.
68. *The Books in My Life*, London 1961.

relevant to the literature of our time. From this point of view the work of Momigliano has the undoubted merit of having shown, on the basis of a healthy empiricism, the inadequacy of the various theses tending to seek the origin of biography either in Aristotle and his school, following the indications of Leo, or in the Socratic dialogues (and more precisely in the *Apologia of Socrates*), as Dihle believes[69], or in certain historical situations particularly favourable to the emergence of strong personalities. This last view was that of Ivo Bruns[70] and it reflects the tendency of a certain kind of criticism to approach the historicity of literary phenomena of the ancient world with the categories of a mechanistic historicism. We may wonder up to what point it is correct to define biography not as the description of the facts of a life but as the description of the nature of a personality necessarily considered in the unity of his actions and words[71]. This is a restrictive interpretation which tends to dismiss a whole series of texts undoubtedly relevant to the biographical genre. Certainly no one can deny that the *Apologia of Socrates* is a proper biography, as Dihle has rightly pointed out. But there are also other forms of biography. We should therefore adopt a different approach: biographical narrative varies in relation to the specific functions it assumes in particular historical contexts and in different literary systems. At this point we must share M.I. Finley's astonishment at some theories on the emergence of the notion of individuality both in biography and in portraiture. He writes:

I have never been able to understand how it could be held that Archilochus and the *dramatis personae* of the *Oresteia* were less individual than Socrates (whether Aristophanes', Xenophon's or

69. 1956, p.25.

70. *Das literarische Porträt der Griechen im fünften und vierten Jahrhundert vor Christi Geburt*, Berlin 1896; *Die Persönlichkeit in der Geschichtsschreibung der Alten*, Berlin 1898.

71. Such a presupposition is shared by M.Untersteiner, following Dihle, in his historical survey of biographies of the philosophers which forms a chapter in his latest work, *Problemi di filologia filosofica*, ed.by L.Sichirollo and M.Venturi Ferriolo, Milano 1980, pp.223-247.

Plato's) or Menander's Misanthrope [...] Patently we are faced with a complicated social-psychological-artistic development, not with a simple linear-evolutionary process. A variety of impulses came into play, generated by the complexity of the Greek world at the time, and they did not all pull in the same direction[72].

The unitary vision of the personality was functional in the apologia of Plato (and Socrates himself) which aimed at representing the integrity of a civic behaviour and a moral disposition and the continuity of a doctrine. It was obviously alien to other types of narrative, like that of Theagenes whose purpose was only informative, or that of Ion of Chios with its portraitistic and anecdotical elements, not to mention the Homeric precedents present in the epigrammatic characterizations of some heroes[73] defined by indicating their lineage and the dominant quality of their personalities. Where the constant and variable features of the biographical genre are concerned we must take into consideration already in the archaic age a type of song which Plato classified in the 4th century with the generic term of encomium[74], that is, the song which praises an illustrious man, celebrating his moral virtues and his deeds. The Alexandrians defined it more restrictively, in order to distinguish it from the epinician song, as a convivial song in honour of important personages, worthy of praise[75]. Isocrates too refers to this type of celebrative poetry in the *Evagoras* (5-11), when he claims polemically that he was the first to transfer the encomiastic genre from poetry to prose, a transformation which involves a rejection of the technical instruments of poetry, such as divine intervention in human action, the resources of figurative and

72. 1976, pp.86 and 88.
73. *Il.*3,178 ff. (Agamemnon); 200 ff. (Odysseus); 6,460 f. (Hector). The ancients already saw in these verses the structure typical of the epigram, cf.O.Vox, *Belfagor* 30, 1975, p.67 ff.
74. *Resp.* 10,607a.
75. As we see from the early quotations of the verses of Bacchylides and Pindar, which the Alexandrians had classified as *encomia*: cf.Bacchyl.frr.20-21 Sn.-Maehl.; Pind.frr.118-120 Sn.-Maehl. This is a poetic genre which had been designated with the term *skólia* (table verses) in the pre-Alexandrian age. Cf.A.E.Harvey, *Class.Quart.* n.s.5, 1955, p.162 ff.

81

metaphorical language, and the harmony of meter and rhythm, and requires greater adherence to the spoken language of the poet's own city. By removing the subliminal and mystifying effect of the poetic language, this procedure necessarily brings the mind back to the truth of the facts. In this sense, the didactic narrative of Isocrates takes its place alongside that of Euripides, Thucydides and Plato in vindicating the principle of the true and the useful as opposed to the hedonistic objective of poetic expression[76], with the notable difference that Isocrates explains the deforming power of poetry with its metalinguistic character connected with the use of neologisms, of words alien to common usage, of figurative and metaphorical expressions. Here the implicit reference is to that very power of illusion and magic suggestion of the poetic word which was justified by Gorgias[77], but which Isocrates rejects in the name of the true and the useful. The new position of Isocrates, like that of Thucydides and, later, of Plato, was founded on the theoretical premise of the greater validity of the written narrative which excluded the notion of 'pleasure' and 'delight' (*hēdonē*) as exercised on the audience by the word united to song, gesture and dance[78]. His attitude fits into the new system of written communication which triumphs over the culture of oral communication between the end of the 5th and the beginning of the 4th century.

If we see them in this perspective, we can elucidate the distinctive features of the *Evagoras*. In analyzing the work as a literary genre, ancient criticism already noted its peculiar character at the borders of the encomium and the funeral oration[79]. If, in as much as it was supposed to celebrate a dead person, the narrative can be regarded as a funeral oration, it nevertheless lacks two of the 'generic' elements, the lament and the consolation, which would have appeared improper because of the long time which had elapsed since the death of Evagoras and the not im-

---

76. Above, p.11 ff.
77. Fr.82 B 11,9 ff. D.-K.
78. Isocr.*Panath*.10-11, cf. p.15 f.
79. Cf.the *Hypóthesis*.

mediately funerary purpose of the work, regarded by its author rather as an ethical-political exhortation addressed to Nicocles, the dead man's son. For these reasons the denomination constantly adopted by Isocrates himself is 'encomium' or 'eulogy'[80] — an eulogy which distinguishes itself from the traditional poetic encomium by the exactitude and concreteness of the biographical references to a great contemporary who had restored Greek culture to Salamis in Cyprus of which he was the sovereign, transforming his fellow citizens from barbarians to Greeks[81], and thus accomplishing a true work of civilization. It is an encomium *sui generis*, and thus also a biography. The physical and moral qualities of the adolescent Evagoras, his noble and heroic descent going back to the Aeacidai, his intellectual gifts and his conduct in the exercise of power and the wars he fought are all linked to form a systematic biographic narrative the chief function of which is not only educative and useful to Nicocles, but also politically useful for the pan-Hellenic ideal of Isocratean propaganda. The boast, expressed by Isocrates in another work[82], of being superior to Pindar as a writer of encomium, is not fortuitous. We therefore have an encomiastic biography which leads, in its structure and attitude, directly to the conception of biography as an autonomous text with an encomiastic function, like the *Life of Philopoemen* by Polybius[83]. In this same tradition developed by Isocrates Xenophon too takes his place with the *Agesilaus* and the *Cyropaedia*[84]. In the former he raises the problem of whether the treatment of the family origins, of the acts and the virtues of the defunct Spartan king, represents a funeral lamentation (*thrênos*) or rather a true encomium (10,3); just as Isocrates does in the *Evagoras*, he emphasizes the necessarily truthful character of the eulogy addressed to a contemporary (3,1). The

80. *Enkômion*: 8; 11; 73. *Eulogía*: 5; 6; 11; 77. *Épainos*: 3; 5; 6; 73; 77.
81. Especially 66-67.
82. *Antídosis* 166.
83. See above, p.65.
84. On the importance of Isocrates and Xenophon for the history of biography, see Osley 1946, p.9.

Cyropaedia is notoriously difficult to classify as several 'generic' features of the history, the eulogy and the pedagogic treatise seem to converge. The intention of revealing in the biographic narrative the deep reasons for the extraordinary governmental capacities of the protagonist emerges fully in the author's programmatic declarations (1,1,6). This is a novel about real life rather than a novelized biography (as it has sometimes been defined).

In these pages we have endeavoured to clarify the idea of biography in Greek thought already implicit in the concrete activity of the earliest authors, but explicitly theorized in later times when biography was already institutionalized as a "genre", that is, when, in a bookish civilization, writing was felt to be a *literary* act. The line we have tried to follow implies the acknowledgment of the principle, held by the most open and perceptive critics, that the differential quality of any literary work depends: a) on its function; b) on the correlation of its constitutive elements with the series of similar elements in other systems and other series. The discussion of biography should be inserted in a wider discussion of literary genres of ancient Greece. We should avoid any excessive schematism which stiffens the differential 'generic' features, and keep our eye on their functional flexibility and the generative and dialectic processes which represent the historicity of the literary act. An incontrovertible fact where ancient Greece is concerned, is that we cannot speak of a systematic theory of literary genres before the classification effected by Hellenistic philology in the 3rd — 2nd century B.C. Practical, technical and organizational requirements, connected with the activity of editors and librarians, induced the Alexandrian grammarians to classify the works of the poets of the past in genres and sub-genres, according to the necessity of dividing them into various *volumina*[85]. It is in the cultural climate of Hellenistic philology, as we have seen, that the biographical pamphlet assumes the status of a literary genre though still retaining its organic relationship with

85. Cf.Pfeiffer 1968, p.171 ff. and especially p.183.

historiography. In this respect the theorization of Polybius is particularly significant. We can conclude this brief discussion of the idea of biography with the appropriate words of S. Mazzarino[86]:

Once again: the opposition between the literary genres *historía* and *bíos* should not be 'pressed' beyond certain limits.

86. 1966, II/2 p.138.

APPENDIX I

THE PONTIFICAL CHRONICLE

In an almost complementary relationship to the still prevalent oral mode of communication, there developed in Rome what might almost be called an archival interest in compiling by means of written documents accessible to a restricted group of readers a precise record of past events[1]. This is no less than an orientation towards history on the part of Roman culture, not only where family traditions are concerned, but also on the official level of civic chronicles, the composition of which constituted, along with the *Fasti consulares*, one of the institutional tasks of the pontifical college. To begin with at least the registration of the most important facts relating to civil life and to military campaigns was regarded as a sacred and esoteric activity.

In its genesis and in the specificity of its forms and content, however, this pontifical chronicle has represented one of the most arduous problems of archaic Latin culture, around which have developed masses of theories and hypotheses not always supported by evidence. In view of this awkward premise, it would be absurd to formulate further hypotheses or to proceed with a tedious and otiose reexamination of those of others. Instead, we shall rely on the few testimonies available and, by way of critical evaluation, derive information which is certain, even if circumscribed and limited, about the nature and the vicissitudes of the pontifical annals[2]. We do not of course mean to

1. On the documentary archives belonging to the principal Roman families, cf. the statement by Pliny *N. H.* 35, 7: *Tabulina codicibus implebantur et monimentis rerum in magistratu gestarum.*
2. Of the vast literature on the subject, we shall only refer to the studies of major importance which we have used in the course of this chapter: Peter 1914, p. III ff.; Cantarelli 1898, p. 209 ff.; F. Altheim, *Epochen der röm. Gesch.* II,

answer an excessive confidence in mere hypotheses with an equally sterile scepticism which would ultimately prove to be no more than polemical and negative.

We learn from Cicero[3] that in a remote epoch history was merely the composition of annals supervised by the Pontifex Maximus. It consisted of a written compilation of every event that occurred year by year from the origins to the pontificate of P. Mucius Scaevola, i.e. until c. 130-114 B.C. This annual record was then transcribed by the Pontifex himself on a tablet publicly exposed in the Regia for everyone to see. This was chronicle-like material which, Cicero tells us, was still *Annales Maximi* in his day. From the rest of his discussion relevant to the comparison between Greek and Roman historiography of the origins, it appears that the information recorded by the Pontifices generally concerned the times, men, places and events, in other words those same elements proper to a historical narrative.

The testimony of Servius[4] completes the information and fills in certain details: each year the Pontifex Maximus had a white tablet (*tabula dealbata*) on which, after having written the names of the consuls and of the other magistrates, he noted down day by day all that was worthy of being remembered concerning either the internal vicissitudes of the city or military actions. Already in the archaic age this constant and diligent daily work of registration furnished the material for a vast collection in 80 volumes called *Annales Maximi* because they were drawn

Frankfurt a. Main 1935, p. 298 ff.; J. E. A. Crake, *Class. Philol.* 35, 1940, p. 375 ff.; F. Jacoby, *Atthis*, Oxford 1949, p. 60 ff.; De Sanctis 1956, p. 15 ff.; Pareti 1952, p. 13 ff.; Fraccaro 1957, p. 59 ff.; Momigliano 1966, p. 59 ff.; E. Badian, in *Latin Historians*, ed. by T. A. Dorey, London 1966, p. 1 ff.; Mazzarino 1966, II/1 pp. 250 ff.; 261 ff.; Gabba 1966, p. 149 ff.; Musti 1970, pp. 27-29; Peruzzi 1973, pp. 175-208. For a systematic discussion of the various contributions on the problem of the pontifical annals, see A. Alföldi, *Early Rome and the Latins*, Ann Arbor 1963 [1965], and G. Perl, *Forsch. u. Fortschr.* 38, 1964, pp. 185 ff.; 213 ff. For the texts, cf. Peter 1914, pp. III ff.; 3 f.; *F. Gr. Hist.* 840 F 1-5.

3. *De or.* 2, 12, 52 = Peter 1914, p. III f. = *F. Gr. Hist.* 840 F 2a.

4. Serv. Dan. *ad Aen.* 1, 373 = Peter 1914, p. IV = *F. Gr. Hist.* 840 F 2b.

from the work of the Pontifices Maximi.

One fact that emerges from Cicero and Servius is the clear distinction, already observed in the last century by T.H. Dyer and L. Cantarelli[5], between: a) *commentarii* or notes gathered privately by the Pontifex and preserved in the archives of the *Regia*; b) *tabula dealbata*, whose purpose was to make public part, if not all, of the notes of the Pontifex; c) *Annales Maximi*, that is the official[6] and definitive edition in 80 volumes, edited towards the end of the 2nd century B.C. by Mucius Scaevola or by others[7], of all the chronicle material in the archives of the Pontifices. If we are to believe Cicero the pontifical records began with the history of Rome itself, as we see in the late Roman author of the *Origo gentis Romanae*[8] who states that the fourth book of the pontifical annals narrated the legends of Alba and the Alban kings. But it is evident that Cicero was basing himself solely on the *Annales Maximi*, which did include a section on the origins. Cicero does not, then, provide independent evidence for determining the epoch in which the recording actually began, and it obviously cannot be traced back to such a remote age.

One point of reference has been recognized in the solar eclipse of c.403 B.C., which, according to the explicit testimony of Cicero[9], was mentioned in Ennius[10] and in the *Annales Maximi*[11]

---

5. Dyer, *The History of the Kings of Rome*, London 1868, p. XXIX f.; Cantarelli 1898, p. 209 ff.

6. Cicero (*De rep.* 2, 15, 28) emphasizes the official character of the *Annales Maximi* qualifying them as *annales publici* (cf. also Diomed. *Gr. Lat.* I, p. 484 Keil = Peter 1914, p. XVII n. 3).

7. According to Cicero (*De or.* 2, 12, 52; cf. n. 3), the custom of registering the most important events year by year and transcribing them on the *tabula* ended with the pontificate of P. Mucius Scaevola; Servius (*loc. cit.* n. 4) affirms that the ancients (*veteres*) had already edited the collection of the pontifical commentaries in 80 volumes. From the combination of the two testimonials it has been deduced that the editor of the *Annales Maximi* was really P. Mucius Scaevola.

8. 17, 3; 5.

9. *De rep.* 1, 16, 25.

10. *Ann.* 153 Skutsch (163 Vahlen).

11. Fr. 3 Peter[2].

and was the starting point for the calculation of the preceding eclipses as far back as the age of Romulus[12]. If we were also to use Livy's reference[13] to the speech of the tribune Canuleius, the *terminus ante quem* for the composition of the commentaries of the Pontifices could be extended to 445 B.C. Canuleius is supposed to have lamented the fact that the plebes were not allowed to consult the *fasti* and the commentaries of the Pontifices lest they advance political claims, basing their requests on a precise knowledge of past events. That Numa Pompilius had become king without being a patrician or a Roman citizen could thus constitute a political precedent for the plebes' claim to the consulate. But Canuleius adds, not without irony, that in spite of the patricians' claim to keeping it secret, certain information was naturally known through oral tradition not only to all the Romans, but also to foreigners. This testimony is of decisive significance for evaluating the effect of oral tradition on the later literary annals and on Greek historiography of the earliest period of Rome. In our opinion, on the other hand, it is not of such importance for fixing the *terminus post quem* of the public exposition of the *tabula dealbata*, as Cantarelli suggested[14]: the publication in itself does not seem in total contrast with the secrecy of the commentaries since, as we shall see, it was easy to conceal circumstances and political implications which might compromise the prestige of the upper class.

12. Cf. De Sanctis 1956, p. 19 f. Cicero (*De rep.* 1, 16, 25) affirms that, according to Ennius, the eclipse occurred about the year 350 of the Roman era (*anno quinquagesimo CCC fere post Romam conditam*). Because of this Pareti (1952, p. 14) maintained that the date of the eclipse must have been calculated not from 753 B. C., but from c.880, i.e. from the year of the foundation of Rome according to Ennius' chronology, and thus fixed around 530 B. C. Beloch, on the other hand, who believes that the pontifical annotations started towards the beginning of the 3rd cent. B. C., proposed emending the reading *quinquagesimo CCC*, transmitted by the manuscript of *De republica*, to *quinquagesimo CCCC* and to identify the eclipse with the one that occurred in 288 B. C. (*Hermes* 57, 1922, p. 119 ff.; *Röm. Gesch.*, Berlin-Leipzig 1926, p. 92 f.). On Beloch's hypothesis, cf. Fraccaro 1957, p. 62 and Mazzarino 1966, II/1 p. 271 ff. who nevertheless defends the transmitted text and declares himself in favour of the traditional interpretation.

13. 4, 3, 9.

14. 1898, p. 214.

But this information, in any case, has a purely orientative value. We cannot really exclude the possibility that the annalistic practice, at least where the composition of commentaries for private use is concerned, goes back to a more remote epoch[15].

As regards the content of these pontifical chronicles, the earliest testimony we have, that of Cato, has generally appeared in marked contrast to the statements of Cicero and Servius. In the fourth book of the *Origines* Cato declares that he does not like to dwell in his historical narrative on facts registered in the tablet of the Pontifex Maximus (*quod in tabula apud pontificem maximum est*), like the price of grain and the eclipses of the moon or of the sun, topics of such futility as not to be worth his attention[16]. From these explicit and polemical words of Cato we might infer that the pontifical tablets were limited to information of practical interest concerning the requirements of commercial and agricultural life, and that they neglected all other news about the major events in political life and military campaigns. But this presumed discrepancy is a mere hypothesis, supported by neither of the two possible interpretations of Cato's text. Either Cato intended to refer polemically only to some of the information furnished by the pontifical tablets, that is, to

15. The information given by Livy (1, 60, 3) about commentaries written by Servius Tullius is problematic. Still less credible is the other piece of information, also by Livy (1, 32, 2), about commentaries by King Numa, from which Ancus Marcius would have ordered the Pontifex to extract the norms concerning the sacred law (*sacra publica*) and expose them on a tablet. On the other hand we cannot confirm this testimony with the discovery, in 181 B. C., of the presumed sepulchre of Numa containing an ark with legal-wisdom writings on papyrus, some in Latin, others in Greek, on the true nature of which the sources disagree. The writings were explicitly attributed to Numa himself by an inscription placed on the ark. For the perplexities and doubts about the authenticity of these writings, see the lucid analyses by W. Speyer, *Bücherfunde in der Glaubenswerbung der Antike*, Göttingen 1970, pp. 51-55 (with bibliography); *Die literarische Fälschung im heidnischen und christlichen Altertum*, München 1971, pp. 67 f.; 89 f.; 141 f. and by F. Della Corte, 'Numa e le streghe', *Maia* 26, 1974, pp. 3-20. Ready to acknowledge authenticity is Peruzzi 1973, pp. 15 f.; 107-144.

16. *Ap.* Gell. 2, 28, 6 = fr. 77 Peter².

those elements he considered futile and lacking historical interest[17], or else even if the matters he mentioned were all that was registered on the tablets, this limitation may well have applied only to the *tabula dealbata* and not to the *commentarii* of which the *tabula* contained a shorter version destined to bring to public notice exclusively the events of practical and immediate interest[18]. If, as we have sought to show, this presumed discrepancy does not exist, we must give up the hypothesis of a reelaboration of the annals in the epoch in which they were published — a reelaboration made to complete the annalistic chronical with political and military information. It was a hypothesis which served only to explain how Cicero and Servius could allude to topics that do not appear in Cato[19].

If the critical line we have followed is correct, the greater part of the material used in the *Annales Maximi* must have consisted of the commentaries of the Pontifices which probably represented an ampler and more particularized version than the *tabulae*[20]. If there really was a reelaboration, it should probably be placed, as Pareti has rightly realized[21], during the period im-

17. The mixture of political-military information and information about prodigies and eclipses could be confirmed by the comparison used by Peter (1914, p. XXV ff.) with the chronicle annotations of the *tabulae paschales*, written in the Middle Ages and preserved in churches and monasteries.

18. Even if many details of the compilation of the commentaries and the *tabulae* can obviously not be checked, the reconstruction proposed by Cantarelli (1898, p. 209 ff.) appears probable. The annotations were probably registered first in the commentaries in a more ample form, and then, in a more condensed form, on the *tabula*. This had to be exposed at the *Regia* not at the end, but at the beginning of the year, in such a way that the most important facts were noted by the Pontifex as they occurred for the purpose of furnishing the citizens with immediate information. Once they had been withdrawn at the end of the year, the tablets were not preserved in the *Regia*. The contrary hypothesis, maintained by Pareti (1952, p. 13), does not seem likely if only for reasons of space (cf. Fraccaro 1957, p. 61). Moreover if the commentaries were preserved in the archive, there would have been no point in preserving the tablets.

19. Cf. most recently Momigliano 1966, p. 59 f.

20. On the writing surface on the *tabula* and on the extent of the text it contained, see the convincing observations of Peruzzi (1973, p. 187 f.).

21. 1952, p. 14 f.

mediately after the Gallic Fire (c. 390 B.C.). In this connection, Livy's precise and circumstantial discussion[22] of documentation available to him for the composition of the first five books of his *Histories* is of supreme importance. Livy remarks that his narrative of the events of the earliest age of Rome from the origins up to the Gallic Fire lacks documentary bases as solid as those for the later period. He provides various reasons: in the first place the distance in time, which makes the facts of a distant past appear more obscure; in the second place the rarity of writing in remote antiquity and the consequent necessity for the historian to trust in oral traditions; and finally — and this is the point of greatest interest to us — the disappearance of the larger part of the pontifical commentaries and other documents from public and private archives which were destroyed in the Gallic Fire of Rome[23]. Livy's attitude is more confident when narrating later events, as if he were setting out to write the history of Rome starting from a second foundation of the city[24].

After the Gallic Fire had destroyed a large part of the archival material, says Livy[25], it was felt necessary to locate the surviving texts of laws and treaties and to rewrite the irremediably lost documents, as the annalist Clodius attests for the genealogical tablets[26]: the new version contains forgeries reflecting the interests of whoever wanted to join the nobility. We may well

22. 6, 1.
23. De Sanctis' scepticism (1956, p. 4 f.) about the ancient testimonials of the destruction of public and private documents in the Gallic fire appears unjustified. We do not see why a piece of information on which the sources agree need be an "etiological myth" destined to explain the scarcity of ancient documents still accessible toward the end of the republican era. Recently Peruzzi (1973, p. 202 f.) has supposed that the *volumina* containing the commentaries of the Pontifices had in some way been saved, as happened to other sacred objects of public interest, which, according to Livy, were partly hidden underground and partly transferred to Caere before the Gauls entered Rome (5, 40, 7-10; cf. also 5, 39, 9-11; 5, 50, 3; 7, 20, 7). A large part of the documents may indeed have been saved, but what we wish to emphasize is that not *all* the documents could have been.
24. 6, 1, 3: *clariora deinceps certioraque ab secunda origine velut ab stirpibus laetius feraciusque renatae urbis gesta domi militiaeque exponentur.*
25. 6, 1, 10.
26. *Ap.* Plut. *Numa* 1, 2 = fr. 1 Peter[2].

assume that, just when the compilation of the annual chronicle began again, much the same thing happened to the commentaries of the Pontifices which had, as we saw, been largely destroyed in the fire[27]. The ways and means by which the Pontifices elaborated this new version are easy to imagine. Besides turning to their mnemonic repertory and to the oral traditions which constituted one of the fundamental historical sources for the reconstruction of the past in that period, they must also have used every other surviving document, public or private. To that occasion, then, just when the pontifical chronicle seemed to revive together with the city of Rome itself, we may attribute the writing of that part of the commentaries relating to the period of the origins which was then included in the first books of the *Annales Maximi*[28].

The reelaboration of the pontifical chronicle, like that of the

27. The hypothesis appears obvious, nor can the argument *ex silentio* adopted by Fraccaro (1957, p. 62) against it be decisive. He insists, as against Pareti, on the lack of testimonials concerning the reconstitution of "historical works" after the fire of Rome.

28. Though slight modifications and manipulations at the time of the publication of the *Annales Maximi* cannot be excluded, it is nevertheless impossible to believe that entire books on the origins and the regal age were added when these topics had already been treated in the literary annals. Besides, the purpose of the publication was obviously to make known in a definitive edition the age-old activity of the Pontifices once the custom of the annual commentaries had ended. In this connection the statement of Dionysius of Halicarnassus (1, 74, 3) could have a decisive value; according to him, Polybius (6, 11a, 2) must have relied for the date of the foundation of Rome on the unique testimony of the pontifical tablet. Even if the chronology of the composition of the works of Polybius is very problematic, in particular that of book VI (cf. A. Lesky, *Gesch. gr. Lit.*, Bern 1971³, p. 866 f., with bibliography), we can nevertheless presume with almost absolute certainty that it was written before the publication of the *Annales Maximi*. It would thus prove that, before the edition of the *Annales Maximi*, part of the pontifical documents was on the period of the origins. It stands to reason that if the testimony of Dionysius is thus understood, the expression ἐπὶ τοῦ παρὰ τοῖς ἀρχιερεῦσι κειμένου πίνακος must, because of the above considerations, be interpreted as a general reference to the pontifical archives. If, on the other hand, Polybius found the date *ab urbe condita* on the tablet that was still exposed in his day from year to year outside the *Regia* (cf. Peruzzi 1973, p. 200), Dionysius' testimony would be of no use for dating the part of the *Annales Maximi* about the origins.

genealogical tables, was not, of course, free of tendentious alterations inspired by the financial and political interests of the Pontifices or even by those same ambitions of the nobility which Cicero had already denounced as a cause of historical falsification in the *laudationes funebres*[29].

29. *Brut.* 16, 62. Mazzarino (1966, II/1 p. 250) observes rightly: "Pontifices belonging to a particular political group of noblemen can have added convenient information to complete other information which did not satisfy them". A relevant example of such a procedure is noted by Mazzarino in the juxtaposition of the episode of the plebeian Lucius Albinius, the sacred saviour of Rome at the time of the Gallic catastrophe, and the two other aristocratic versions which present Camillus and M. Manlius Capitolinus as the military and political saviours of Rome.

APPENDIX II

ON LITERARY GENRES

The result of our investigation into the typologies of historical and biographical narrative in ancient culture leads us to reconsider the problem of 'genres' in the poetry and prose of the Greeks in terms of the phenomenology of communication. This brief appendix describes the methodological premises on which our analysis is based and our view of the essential points of this problem.

We believe, to start with, that literary genres represent a communicative system within the structure of literary communication. They reflect the most conservative and lasting tendencies in the development of literature, and their conservation capacity is in direct relation to their capacity of being renewed in each individual work in the function of new cultural realities. As an institution, the genre is always old and new because it lives in the present and, at the same time, recalls the past and its origins. This perspective permits us to find the constant elements in the literary system — narrative structures, techniques of exposition, key concepts of narrative — without ever losing sight of the historical process or the continuous contribution of the significant variants. It is the problem of the relationship between literature and public, a dialectic resolved either in a full correspondence between the work and the expectations of those for whom it is intended or in a radical break between the two, which the critic must define in its semantic dimension and its historical genesis[1]. As we know, genre theory has passed through

1. See in this respect the concept of "horizon of expectation" in the public, theorized by H. R. Jauss, *Literaturgeschichte als Provokation der Literaturwissenschaft*, Konstanz 1967.

97

numerous vicissitudes according to the various epochs of European culture. Apart from the heated discussions and polemics on the subject in the Renaissance and Baroque periods, its most ample analytic development occurred in the general theory of literature elaborated by positivism and in a negative critical tendency of idealism. Both perspectives contained a margin of equivocation in the definition of the genres, the first representing them according to the model of a biological species in evolution[2], the second seeing them as pure and simple abstract entities, subsumed after the event by criticism. One made of the genre a biological reality circumscribed in the individuality of its species and evolving in time according to the Darwinian principle, while the other made of it an empirical-abstract scheme unable to catch the essence of a literary work. These two unilateral perspectives do not take into account the pragmatic vision of the genre and its communicative function.

Beyond the two opposed conceptions of literary genre as an objective reality of a naturalistic type which has always contained the organic principle of its evolution, or as an abstract scheme elaborated after the event for descriptive purposes, the research of the Russian formalists had the merit of studying genre in a structural vision of the work and the literary institutions. This position allows us to grasp the specific quality of the genre, the function peculiar to each formal element and the appearance of new functions as they are fulfilled in the relationship between the traditional system and the modern message[3]. The evolutionism of Brunetière, who theorized the action of the work on the work, is thus revived in the sense of the innate dynamism in the relationship between individual message and literary system.

The theory elaborated by Russian formalism is actually the sole instrument which permits a full understanding, in both a

2. Typical is the position of F. Brunetière, *L'évolution des genres dans l'histoire de la littérature*, Paris 1890.
3. Ju. N. Tynjanov, *Archaisty in novatory*, Leningrad 1929 = *Avanguardia e tradizione*, It.trans. Bari 1968.

synchronic and diachronic perspective, of the phenomenon of literary genres in ancient Greece. It is not by chance that Bakhtin[4] reached the definition of the serio-comic genre which he applied to 19th century Russian narrative starting from the study of ancient literature and, in particular, from the Platonic dialogue. The category was already clearly present in the critical reflection of the Greeks through the notion of *psógos* and *geloîon*, that is, of a work of poetry or prose which mingles blame and jest, situating itself at the opposite pole to the encomium[5]. It is surprising, and has never been sufficiently emphasized, that Bakhtin's intuition about the Platonic dialogue, seen by him as a typical example of the serio-comic, finds a significant precedent in ancient thought. After having read Plato's dialogue bearing his name Gorgias said: "How Plato can mock (ἰαμβίζειν)". After he had dedicated his own gold statue at Delphi, Plato hailed him when he saw him and addressed him ironically: "Behold Gorgias handsome and all of gold". And Gorgias replied: "Handsome and new is the Archilochus that Athens has begot!"[6]. Gorgias saw in the curious mixture of seriousness and facetiousness that characterizes the dialogue a precise element of continuity with the poetic genre that had its most representative exponent in Archilochus.

If we now turn to Greek culture in its earliest phase up to the 5th century B.C., which was primarily oral, we see a combination of various poetic genres operating on a pragmatic level rather than on the level of the apparent structure of the work and its internal organization. Song depended on the various occasions of social life and the type of vocal and instrumental performance required on each occasion. This particular sociological component of Greek culture in its pre-bookish phase has not received adequate emphasis from those who have treated the problem of the ancient literary genres.

4. *Dostoevsky. Poetica e stilistica*, It. trans. Torino 1948, p. 140; 'Epos e romanzo. Sulla metodologia dello studio del romanzo', in *Problemi di teoria del romanzo*, Torino 1976, p. 200 ff.

5. Aristot. *Poet*. 1448 b.

6. Athen. 11, 505 d-e; Gorg. 82 A 15a D.-K.

Fundamental for the earliest history of the lyric genres is a passage in the *Laws*[7] in which Plato argues against the license in his time in treating the traditional musical norms which had until then marked the dividing line between the various types of poetry: in ancient times, he says, *mousikē* was divided into genres and defined modes, which characterized respectively the hymns to the gods, the funeral laments (*thrēnoi*), the *nómoi* for lyre and other forms of song, such as the paean in honour of Apollo and the dithyramb in honour of Dionysus. It was not permissible to transgress this distinction between performances, abusively substituting one type of melody for another. According to Plato the political authorities should ensure a rigorous respect for the poetical-musical tradition, and the public itself should listen in silence, without disturbing the performance by whistling or applause as happened in Plato's day. In the new situation attacked by Plato, the new poets, vying to please an unruly public that fancied itself a good judge of poetry, confused the features peculiar to the various genres of their performances.

This passage of Plato is significant for two reasons. In the first place, it shows that division into genres had operated in Greek culture of the archaic and classical period even within the substantial unity of the melic production denominated by the comprehensive term "hymn"[8]. This term, we should stress, assumes in Plato[9] the specific significance of a prayer to the gods as opposed to a song in honour of men (*enkōmion*), performed before the restricted audience of a symposium or the vaster audience of a solemn ceremony in honour of an athlete who had triumphed in the agonic feasts. In the second place, the

7. 3, 700b ff.
8. An ample documentation of the term is to be found in all archaic poetry. For hymn in the sense of *thrēnos* cf. Anacr. fr. 168 Gent.; Aesch. *Pers.* 620; 626; *Ag.* 709 etc.; in the generic sense of "symposium song" cfr. above all Anacr. fr. 33, 11 Gent.; Xenophan. fr. 1,13 Gent.-Pr.; Teogn. 993; in the sense of song of celebration of an agonic victory it is frequently used in Bacchylides and Pindar.
9. *Resp.* 10, 607 a.

passage documents a state of crisis which affected the traditional genres between the 5th and the 4th century, both in the melic forms and in the content. The true objective of Plato's polemic was really the composite style of the so-called new dithyramb which, with free use of harmonies in the three different genres (enharmonic, diatonic and chromatic), had affected every other melic form[10]. With Timotheus, music certainly reached the highest point of mimetic expressivity, as we infer both from the testimonials of contemporaries[11] and from the lexical and stylistic audacities of the poetic text. The triumph of the new dithyramb coincides with the final affirmation of writing and prose activities, submitted to the meditated control of the writer. The new art, open to the most daring musical experiments, limited the role of the verbal text to the point of reducing it to a mere *text for music*. With the decline of orality and its energies innate in the charm of the execution, the new music was able to replace that suggestive and emotional power characteristic of oral poetry with the mimetic force of its experimentation.

But Plato[12] also elaborates on a theoretical level a typology of narrative that permits him to classify poetic production in three large categories based on the internal structure of the work: 1) 'simple' narrative in the third person; 2) mimetico-dialogical narrative; 3) mixed narrative. To the first genre he assigns the dithyramb, conceived as a song of the chorus which narrates mythical events; to the second dramatic poetry, tragic and comic; to the third, finally, the epic and other genres which contain narrative and dialogue. With the expression 'other genres' he evidently means all those poematic forms, iambic, elegiac and lyric, in which narrative and dialogical parts coexist. This is confirmed by the further classification into sub-genres developed by

---

10. Dion. Hal. *De comp. verb.* 29 (II p. 85 f. Us.-Rad.), cf. Ps. Plut. *De mus.* 4, 1132de.
11. Pherecr. fr. 145,19 K. (*ap.* Ps. Plut. *De mus.* 30, 1141f) = Test. 10 Del Grande.
12. *Resp.* 3, 392d-394c.

the grammarian Diomedes[13], still within the bounds of the three fundamental genres of the Platonic doctrine: dramatic or active, exegetical-narrative, and common. This last, i.e. the mixed genre with a combination of dramatic and narrative structure, includes, along with epic, the lyric poetry exemplified by Archilochus and Horace.

The theory of genre elaborated by the Alexandrian scholars follows in the wake of Plato's rhetorical theory. The contexts and the situations to which the poetry of the past was destined were disappearing; poetry was from then on read as literature *tout court* and, consequently, classified not on the basis of the original pragmatic criteria but according to internal criteria of a rhetorical type, based on the structure of the work and its contents. Hence the abstract individuation of genres and subgenres, which often gave rise to uncertainties and disputes in the classification of single texts of archaic and late-archaic poetry, as documented, for example, by the controversy between Callimachus and Aristarchus over the classification of the *Cassandra* of Bacchylides. This seemed a dithyramb to Aristarchus, while Callimachus maintained that it was a paean, basing his judgment on the ritual cry *ié* which recurred in the poem[14].

The classification of the genres in the Alexandrian age was substantially bookish not only in its analytical formulation but also in its genesis and its operative ends in as much as it was narrowly linked to the practical necessities of critical editing and the libraries. Conceived with the principal purpose of offering a rational catalogue of ancient texts, this doctrine of genres ended by exercising a decisive influence on the literary taste of the time, which expressed itself, on the critical level, in a complex and elaborate theoretical structure and, on the concrete level of poetic activity, in the tendency towards a sophisticated contamination and mixture of poetic genres[15].

13. *Gr. Lat.* I, p. 482 f. Keil.
14. *Schol.* Bacchyl. *Carm.* 22-23, p. 127 f. Sn.-Maehl.
15. On the poetic genres in ancient Greece, see the fundamental work of H. Färber, *Die Lyrik in der Kunsttheorie der Antike*, München 1936, and the arti-

cle of A. E. Harvey, *Class. Quart.* n.s. 5, 1955, pp. 161-174. The successive attempts at theoretical reassessment should be kept in mind: L. E. Rossi, *Bull. Inst. Class.Stud. Univ. London* 18, 1971, p. 69 ff.; C. Calame, *Quad. Urb.* 17, 1974, p. 113 ff.; M. Fantuzzi, *Lingua e stile* 25, 1980, p. 433 ff.; D. Lanza, *Quad. Urb.* n.s. 13 (42), 1983, p. 51 ff. In the discussion of genres in Greek culture it is of primary importance to understand the changing course of the archaic situation whose dislocation into genres was closely connected with the different occasions and modes of execution, without implicating the internal structure of the work, until the new situation in the 4th century when classification was based on this last criterion. For this essential passage, see B. Gentili, Epigramma ed elegia', in *L'Épigramme grecque, Entret. Hardt* XIV, Vandoeuvres-Genève 1967, p. 39 ff.; Gentili 1972, p. 57 ff.

103

APPENDIX III

TOWARDS A CORRECT INTERPRETATION OF «PHRASAI» IN THE FRAGMENT OF DURIS

Duris' criticism of the historical work of Ephorus and Theopompus deserves further consideration. He claims that their interest was primarily aimed at the 'written page' (*gráphein*), neglecting the delight intrinsic in the aural dimension of the word (ἡδονὴ ἐν τῷ φράσαι), i.e. the emotional reflexes provoked by the declamation of the text. Our interpretation may arouse a certain perplexity where the sense it attributes to the term *phrásai* ("say", "declaim") is concerned. Indeed, the corresponding substantive, *phrásis,* usually has the generic meaning of "elocution", "style"[1], in ancient rhetoric. This semantic connotation is also implicit in Duris' expression, but is decisively orientated towards the style peculiar to a written work for oral communication, as opposed to written work intended instead for silent reading[2].

In his treatise *De compositione verborum,* Dionysius of Halicarnassus used the theory of the rhythmics to examine the structure of some lines of Homer and affirms that the poet manages *with a single meter* (the hexameter) and *with few rhythms*[3] to obtain extraordinary effects of imitative harmony, expressing in the movement of the line the *páthos* inherent in the event described. In his opinion the best example is the holodac-

---

1. Hence, probably, the reductive interpretation of *cultivate style*, which the Greek lexicon of Liddell-Scott-Jones (s.v. φράζω, 2b) also attributes to the φράσαι of our passage.
2. The primary significance of φράζειν, 'say', 'speak', points in this direction.
3. 20, 137-138 (II p. 89 Us.-Rad.)

tylic line of the *Odyssey*[4], describing the stone of Sisyphus rolling downhill:

αὖτις ἔπειτα πέδονδε κυλίνδετο λᾶας ἀναιδής.

He observes that the long syllables of each dactylic foot do not in this case have the normal duration of two beats. Because of the total absence of spondaic feet, whoever recites the line has to assume a *round, rapid and rushing declamation (phrásis)*, like the rolling of the stone[5]. In this context the term *phrásis* certainly indicates the style, but in the specific light of its phonetical-aural aspect[6]. The perspective in which Dionysius places himself is the same one from which Plutarch examines poetry in the opuscule *De audiendis poetis*.

The same significance is found in the adjective used by Aristotle in the section of his *Rhetoric* on the distinction between 'graphic' and 'agonistic' eloquence[7].

4. 11, 598.
5. 20,144 (II p. 93 Us.-Rad.): οὐδὲν δὴ τὸ ἀντιπρᾶττον ἐστὶν εὔτροχον καὶ περιφερῆ καὶ καταρρέουσαν εἶναι τὴν φράσιν ἐκ τοιούτων συγκεκροτημένην ῥυθμῶν. For a more detailed analysis, cf. B. Gentili, *Metrica greca arcaica*, Messina-Firenze 1950, p. 40 ff.
6. L. E. Rossi, *Metrica e critica stilistica. Il termine ciclico e l' ἀγωγή ritmica*, Roma 1963, and W.S. Allen, *Accent and Rhythm*, Cambridge 1973, p. 255 f., rightly observe that Dionysius is dealing with style, but they do not say that the focal point of the analysis is in the stylistic effects on the level of diction or recitation.
7. Aristot. *Rhet.* 3,1407b: ὅλως δὲ δεῖ εὐανάγνωστον εἶναι τὸ γεγραμμένον καὶ εὔφραστον.

INDEX OF SOURCES

fr. 88 B 44 D.-K.: 74 n. 49

DIODORUS SICULUS
20,43,7: 14 n. 29
DIOMEDES
Gr. Lat. I, p. 482 f. Keil: 102
n. 13; p. 484: 89 n. 6
DIONYSIUS OF HALICARNAS-
SUS
Ant. Rom. 1,6: 45 n. 28; 1,8,1-
3: 64 n. 11; 1,74,3: 94 n. 28;
5,48,1: 64 and n. 10; 7,70,1:
49 n. 44; 7,71,1: 49 n. 45
De comp. verb. 20,137-138, II
p. 89 Us.-Rad.: 105 and n. 3;
20,144, II p. 93 Us.-Rad.:
106 and n. 5; 22, II p. 108
Us.-Rad.: 13 n. 24; 29, II p.
85 ff. Us.-Rad.: 101 n. 10
De din. 8: 27 n. 61, 27 n. 64
Epist. ad Pomp. 6, II p. 244 ff.
Us.-Rad.: 16 n. 34, 17 n. 37,
63 n. 5; 6,7, II p. 246,6 Us.-
Rad.: 43 n. 22, 63 n. 7
Opusc. I, p. 340,2 Us.-Rad.:
45 n. 28
DURIS of SAMOS
F. Gr. Hist. 76 F 1: 14 n. 28;
F 67: 24 n. 54; F 70: 24 n.
53

ENNIUS
Ann. fr. 153 Skutsch (163
Vahlen): 89 n. 10
EPHORUS
F. Gr. Hist. 70 F 111: 29 n. 70
EURIPIDES
Med. 190 ff.: 13 n. 25

FABIUS PICTOR
fr. 3 Peter[2]: 48 n. 40; fr. 12:

47 n. 37; fr. 15: 48 n. 42; fr.
16: 48 n. 43; fr. 21 = *F. Gr.
Hist.* 809 T 6a: 38 n. 9; fr.
25 = *F. Gr. Hist.* 809 F 21:
38 n. 10
FANNIUS
fr. 1 Peter[2]: 58 f. and n. 69
F. GR. HIST.
840 F 1-5: 94 n. 2; F 2a: 88
n. 3; F 2b: 88 n. 4; F 24a: 36
n. 2

GELLIUS
2,286: 9a n. 16; 5,18,7-9: 52
f. and n. 56; 11,1,1: 42 n. 19;
11,8,1: 50 n. 48; 11,14: 46
and n. 33
GORGIAS
82 A 15a D.-K.: 99 n. 6; fr. 82
B 11,9 f. D.-K.: 18 and n. 39,
82 n. 77; fr. 82 B 23 D.-K.:
18 n. 40

HECATAEUS OF MILETUS
F. Gr. Hist. 1 F 1: 10 n. 13
HERODOTUS
1,1-5: 9 n. 9; 1,32: 8 n. 5; 2,99:
11 n. 14; 7,152: 11 n. 15
HESIOD
Op. 160: 7 n. 4; 654 ff.: 72 n.
44
fr. 1 Merk.-West: 7 n. 4; fr. 204,
97 ff.: 7 n. 4
HOMER
Il. 3,178 ff.: 81 n. 73; 3,200 ff.:
81 n. 73; 6,640 f.: 81 n. 73;
12,23: 7 n. 4
Od. 11,598: 106 and n. 4
HORACE
Carm. 3,30,1: 13 n. 23

ION OF CHIUS
F. Gr. Hist. 392 F 4 ff.: 69 n.
28; F 6: 69 n. 29; F 12: 70 n.
34; F 13: 70 n. 30; F 15: 70
nn. 31 and 32
ISOCRATES
Ad Nicocl. 48-49: 15 n. 31
Antidosis 166: 83 n. 82
Evag. Hypoth.: 82 n. 79; 3: 83
n. 80; 5: 83 n. 80; 5-11: 81;
6: 83 n. 80; 8: 83 n. 80; 11:
83 n. 80; 66-67: 83 n. 81; 73:
83 n. 80; 77: 83 n. 80
Panath. 10-11: 15 n. 30, 82 n.
78

JOSEPHUS FLAVIUS
Bell. Iud. 1,1-3: 36 n. 5

LIVY
1,32,2: 91 n. 15; 1,60,3: 91 n.
15; 4,3,9: 90 n. 13; 5,39,9-
11: 93 n. 23; 5,40,7-10: 93 n.
23; 5,50,3: 93 n. 23; 6,1: 93
n. 22; 6,1,3: 93 n. 24; 6,1,10:
93 n. 25; 7,20,7: 93 n. 23;
26,24,1-3: 37 n. 7; 31,29-31:
37 n. 8; 39,6,7: 46 n. 34

MANETHO
F. Gr. Hist. 609 F 13: 36 n. 5
MIMNERMUS
fr. 3 Gent.-Pr.: 7 n. 2

NICOLAUS OF DAMASCUS
F. Gr. Hist. 90 F 125-130: 78
n. 64; F 131-139: 78 and n.
63; F 137: 78 n. 64

ORIGO GENTIS ROMANAE
17,3: 89 and n. 8; 17,5: 89 and

n. 8

PAPYRI
P. Oxy. 2506, ed. D. Page: 73
n. 46
PHERECRATES
fr. 145,9 K. = Test. 10 Del
Grande: 101 n. 11
PHOTIUS
Bibl. 176 p. 121a41: 14 n. 29
PINDAR
Nem. 6,6: 8 n. 5
Pyth. 8,95 ff.: 8 n. 5
frr. 118-120 Sn.-Maehl.: 81 n.
75
PLATO
Gorg. 502c: 30 n. 79
Leg. 3,700b ff.: 100 n. 7; 7,
801c-802a: 31 n. 82
Resp. 3,392d-394c: 101 n. 12;
10,595a-607a: 29 and n. 75:
10,597 ff.: 29 n.72; 10,599d:
30 n. 78; 10,601b: 30 n. 79;
10,601d: 29 n. 76; 10,602c:
29 n. 72: 10,602c-608a: 19
n. 42; 10,602d: 29 n. 73, 30
n. 77; 10,605d: 31 n. 80; 10,
607a: 31 n. 81, 81 n. 74, 100
n. 9
Soph. 233b ff.: 29 n. 72
PLAUTUS
Cas. 879: 58 n. 68
Pseud. 387: 58 n. 68
PLINIUS
N.H. 3,57: 36 n.2; 35,7: 87 n.1
PLUTARCH
Alcib. 32: 24 and n. 53
Alex. 1,1: 67; 1,2: 64
Galb. 2,3: 67 n. 19
Nic. 1,1-2: 67
Num. 1,2: 93 n. 26

109

INDEX OF KEY WORDS AND THEMES

- musical, 20 f., 100-102
Gráphein - phrásai, 14 ff., 16 n.
33, 19, 23 and n. 49, 27, 105 f.
Graphiké léxis - agonistiké léxis,
15 f., 27

Hédoné, cf. Usefulness - pleasure
Historiae, cf. Annales - Res gestae
- Historiae
Historical monograph, 51, 57,
65 f.
Historíē, 10
Historikón, 23 and n. 51
Historiographical pessimism, 47
Historiography
- selective, global, 62 ff., 68
- without method (améthodos
hýlē), 23 f. and n. 51, 60
Hýmnos, 100
Hypomnémata, 76, 77

Iambízein, 105; cf. Serio-comic
Iterare, 53, 58 and n. 68

Kephalaiōdós, 45 n. 28, 65
Ktéma, 12 n. 23
Ktíseis, cf. Foundations of cities

Likelihood, 9 f., 19 f., 22 ff., 28
ff.
Linear - cyclic, cf. Cyclic - linear
Linguistic structures, 12-16, 27
f., 50 f., 59 f.
Lyric poetry, 72-75

'Marvellous' in the historical narrative, 16 f., 48 f., 51, 56 f.
Mimesis (mímēsis), 14 f., 14 n.
29, 17 f., 17 n. 35, 19 ff., 20 n.
44, 22, 24 f., 24 n. 55, 29 ff.
Monoeidés, 64

Monumentum, 13 n. 23, 87 n. 1
Music, cf. Genres (musical)
Myth of the origins, 7 f., 26 f.,
35 and n. 1, 44-48, 49, 54 f.,
89

Ophélimon, cf. Usefulness - plea-
sure
Ópsis, cf. Autopsy
Oral tradition, 9-11, 90 f., 92 ff.
Orality, cf. Technology of com-
munication

Párergon, 63
Particular - general, cf. General -
particular
Páthos, 14 n. 29
Performance, 13 and n. 23, 14 n.
27, 18 n. 40, 19
Philarchía, 44
Phrásai - gráphein, cf. Gráphein -
phrásai
Phýsis, 65
Pikría, 63
Plasmatódēs, 57
Pleasure - usefulness, cf. Useful-
ness, pleasure
Pleonexía, 44
Polymorphía, 17, 48, 56, 63
Portrait, 62, 69-73
Pragmatic - apodeictic, cf. Apo-
deictic - pragmatic
Praise, cf. Encomium
Propaganda, cf. Tendentiousness
Próphasis, 11 n. 17
Psógos, 99; cf. Serio-comic

Recital, 1 f., 12 n. 23; cf. Performance
Res gestae, cf. Annales - Res
gestae - Historiae

112

INDEX OF NAMES

Chrysogonus, 24
Cicero, 27, 41, 50, 51, 56, 57, 59, 60, 64, 76, 88, 89, 91, 92, 95
Cimon, 70
Cincius Alimentus, 35, 36, 41, 42, 45, 49
Classen, C.J., 35 n. 1
Clodius, 93
Coelius Antipater, 48 and n. 42, 51, 59, 60
Crake, J.E.A., 88 n. 2
Crates, 23
Critias, 74

Degani, E., 75 n. 53
Della Corte, F., 91 n. 15
De Sanctis, G., 3, 48 n. 39, 88 n. 2, 90 n. 12, 93 n. 23
Dexamenos, 71
Di Benedetto, V., 53 n. 57
Dicaearchus, 73
Diehl, E., 71 n. 38
Dihle, A., 3, 80 and nn. 69 and 71
Dilthey, W., 76
Diocles of Peparethos, 49
Diodorus, 14 n. 29
Diomedes, 102
Dionysius of Halicarnassus, 16, 27, 43, 45, 49, 56, 63, 64, 94 n. 28, 105, 106 and n. 6
Dionysus, 100
Donini, G., 61 n. 1
Dorey, T.A., 88 n. 2
Duris of Samos, 14 and n. 29, 15, 16 and n. 33, 17 and n. 35, 18, 19, 20 and n. 44, 21, 23, 24 and nn. 54 and 55, 27, 49, 105
Dyer, T.H., 89 and n. 5

Egesibulus, 71
Ennius, 38, 44, 89, 90 n. 12
Ephoros, 14, 15, 16, 17 n. 35, 24 and n. 55, 26, 27, 29, 43, 52, 105
Euripides, 13, 14 n. 27, 73 n. 45, 82
Euryptolemus, 24
Evagoras, 82, 83

Fabius Pictor, 35, 36, 38, 39 and n. 11, 40, 41, 42, 43, 45, 47 and n. 37, 48 and n. 42, 49 and n. 47, 52, 54, 55, 57
Färber, H., 102 n. 15
Faini, E., 21 n. 45
Fannius, C., 50, 58
Fantuzzi, M., 103 n. 15
Ferrarotti, F., 75 nn. 51 and 52
Ferrero, L., 44 n. 25
Finley, M.I., 3, 71 n. 37, 80, 81 n. 72
Finnegan, R., 2 n. 3
Folena, G., 8 n. 7
Fornaro, P., 73 n. 45
Forster Smith, C., 10
Fraccaro, P., 3, 88 n. 2, 90 n. 12, 92 n. 18, 94 n. 27
Fraenkel, Ed., 76 n. 56
Fränkel, H., 8 n. 5
Freud, S., 79
von Fritz, K., 3, 17 n. 35, 20 n. 44, 21 n. 47
Furius Purpurio, L., 37

Gabba, E., 3, 35 n. 1, 44 n. 26, 45 nn. 27 and 30, 53 n. 57, 88 n. 2
Galen, 78
Galinski, K., 35 n. 1
Gallo, I., 4, 61 n. 1, 68 n. 22, 69

n. 26
Garofalo, I., 78 n. 65
Gasparri, C., 71 n. 38
Gellius, A., 46, 48 n. 42, 52
Gellius, Cn., 50
Gelzer, M., 4, 32 n. 86, 37 n. 6,
40 n. 14, 44 n. 23, 45 n. 28, 54
nn. 58 and 59
Gentili, B., 4, 7 n. 3, 11 n. 19,
12 n. 20, 13 n. 26, 14 n. 29, 18
n. 40, 19 n. 41, 75 n. 50, 103
n. 15, 106 n. 5
Giangrande, G., 1 *
Gorgias, 18 and n. 40, 23, 82, 99
Gozzoli, S., 64 n. 12
Guardamagna, D., 1 *
Guarducci, M., 1 n. 2
Gugel, H., 68 and n. 25

Hamilcar Barca, 39, 41
Hamilton, A., 1 *
Hanell, K., 4, 36 n. 3, 45 n. 31
Hannibal, 39, 41, 43, 44, 48, 65
n. 16
Harmodius, 71
Harvey, A.E., 81 n. 75, 103 n.
15
Hasdrubal, 38, 39, 41, 43, 44
Havelock, E.A., 4, 12 n. 20, 13
n. 27, 18 n. 38, 19 n. 41
Hecataeus, 10
Hector, 81 n. 73
Hegemon, 75
Herodotus, 10, 11 and n. 17, 12
and n. 22, 14, 36 n. 5, 61, 69
Hesiod, 7, 72
Heurgon, J., 35 n. 1
Hieronymus of Cardia, 36
Hölscher, T., 4, 70 n. 33, 71 n.
37
Homer, 7, 15, 18, 69, 105

Homeyer, H., 61 and n. 2
Horace, 102

Ion of Chios, 69 and n. 28, 70,
71, 81
Ippel, A., 21 n. 45
Isocrates, 14, 15, 16 and n. 33,
18, 20 n. 44, 52, 81, 82, 83
and n. 84

Jacoby, F., 69 n. 28, 78 n. 64,
88 n. 2
Jauss, H.R., 97 n. 1
Josephus Flavius, 36 n. 5, 77

Kaibel, G., 72
Kleberg, T., 13 n. 23
Kresilas, 71
Kritios, 79

Laffranque, M., 11 n. 16
Lanza, D., 103 n. 15
La Penna, A., 4, 44 n. 24, 45 n.
29, 47 n. 35
Lasserre, F., 7 n. 3
Latacz, I., 18 n. 38
Latte, K., 4, 7 n. 4, 10 n. 13, 12
n. 21, 21 n. 47
Leeman, A.D., 47 n. 34, 57 and
n. 64
Lefkowitz, M.R., 14 n. 29, 74 n.
48
Le Goff, J., 25 n. 57
Lejeune, Ph., 77 n. 60
Leo, F., 4, 5, 42 and n. 18, 58 n.
68, 68 n. 23, 73, 76 and nn. 55
and 56, 78 n. 64, 80
Leone, S., 77 n. 61
Lesky, A., 94 n. 28
Levi, M.A., 5, 28 n. 67, 43 n. 21
Licinius, L. Crassus, 60